Collected Later Poems
of Álvaro de Campos

1928-1935

The Pessoa Series from Shearsman Books

Selected English Poems

Mensagem / Message
    (bilingual edition; translated by Jonathan Griffin)

The Collected Poems of Alberto Caeiro
The Collected Later Poems of Álvaro de Campos
    (translated by Chris Daniels)

Lisbon: What the Tourist Should See

Fernando Pessoa – Voices of a Nomadic Soul (by Zbigniew Kotowicz)

Fernando Pessoa

Collected Later Poems
of Álvaro de Campos

(1928-1935)

translated by
Chris Daniels

Shearsman Books

First published in in the United Kingdom in 2009 by
Shearsman Books Ltd
58 Velwell Road
EXETER
EX4 4LD

www.shearsman.com

ISBN 978-1-905700-25-7
First Edition

Contents

Collected Later Poems

1928-1935

Tobacco Shop

I'm nothing.
I'll never be anything.
I can't wish I were anything.
Even so, I have all the dreams of the world in me.

Windows of my room,
Of my room, one of the millions in the world no one knows who owns
(And if they knew, what would they know?),
You open onto the mystery of a street crossed constantly by people,
Onto a street inaccessible to all thought,
Real, impossibly real, certain, unknowably certain,
With the mystery of things beneath stones and beings,
With death putting moisture on walls and gray hairs on men,
With Destiny driving the cart of everything down the road of nothing.

Today I'm vanquished, as if I knew the truth.
Today I'm lucid, as if I were about to die,
And had no more brotherhood with things
Than in a farewell turning that house and that side of the street
Into a row of coaches, a conductor's whistle
From inside my head,
A jolt of nerves and creaking bones in departure.

Today I'm perplexed, like someone who's thought and discovered and lost.
Today I'm divided between the loyalty I owe
The Tobacco Shop across the street, as a real thing outside,
And the feeling that everything's a dream, as a real thing inside.

I've failed in everything.
Since I've proposed nothing, maybe everything was nothing.
The learning they gave me,
I used it to sneak out the back window.
I went to the country with grand intentions,
But all I found there were grass and trees,
And when there were people, they were the same as the others.
I leave the window, sit in a chair. What should I think?

How do I know what I'll be, when I don't even know what I am?
Should I be what I think? But I think about being so many things!
And there are so many thinking they're the same thing—they can't all be!?
Genius? At this moment
A hundred thousand minds like mine dream themselves geniuses like me,
And history won't remember, who knows?, not even one,
Nor will there be anything but the midden of future conquests.
No, I don't believe in myself.
In every asylum there are so many nut-cases with so many certainties!
I, who have no certainties, am I more right or less right?
No, not even in myself…
In how many of the world's garrets and non-garrets
Are there dreaming at this hour how many geniuses-unto-themselves?
So many high and noble and lucid aspirations—
Yes, truly high and noble and lucid—
Who knows if they're plausible—
Will they ever find the light of day, the ears of people?
The world is for those who were born to conquer,
Not for those who dream they can conquer it, even if they're right.
I've dreamed more than Napoleon accomplished.
I've clasped to my hypothetical breast more humanity than Christ ever did.
I've made more philosophies in secret than Kant ever wrote.
But I am, and may always be, the one in the garret,
Even if I don't live in one;
I'll always be *he wasn't born for this*;
I'll always only be *oh, but he had such qualities*;
I'll always be the one who waited for someone to open the door at the
        foot of a doorless wall,
Who sang a ditty of the Infinite in an overgrown field,
Who heard the voice of God in a closed-up well.
Do I believe in myself? No, nor in anything else.
Let Nature pour over my ardent head
Its sun, its rain, the wind that finds my hair
And let the rest come if it comes, or is to come, or doesn't come.
Cardiac slaves of the stars,
We conquer everything before we get out of bed;
But we wake up and it's opaque,

We get up and it's alien,
We go out and it's the entire world,
And then the solar system and then the Milky Way and then the Indefinite.

(Eat chocolates, little girl:
Eat chocolates!
See, there are no other metaphysics in the world beside chocolates.
See, all religions teach no more than a candy store.
Eat, dirty girl, eat!
If only I could eat chocolates as truthfully as you do!
But I think and, tearing the silver paper, which is really only tin foil,
I drop everything on the ground, as I've dropped my life.)

But at least there remains from the sorrow of what I'll never be,
The rapid calligraphy of these verses,
Portico leading into the Impossible.
At least I consecrate to myself a tearless contempt,
At least I'm noble in the grand gesture with which I toss
The dirty clothing I am, without a laundry-list, into the course of things,
And stay home without a shirt.

(You, who console, who do not exist and so console,
Whether Greek goddess, conceived as a statue come to life,
Or Roman patrician, impossibly noble and malignant,
Princess of troubadours, most gentle and colorful,
Marquise of the eighteenth century, décolletée and distant,
Or celebrated coquette of our parent's time,
Or something else modern—I don't know quite what—
All of it, whatever it might be, be it, and let it inspire me if it can!
My heart is an overturned bucket.
As those who invoke spirits invoke spirits I invoke
Me to myself and encounter nothing.
I go to the window and see the street with absolute clarity.
I see the shops, I see the sidewalks, I see the cars pass by,
I see the clothed living entities who cross.
I see the dogs which also exist,
And all of it weighs upon me like a curse of banishment,
And all of it is foreign, as is everything.)

I lived, I studied, I loved, I even believed,
And today there's no beggar I don't envy solely because he's not me.
I see his tatters and his sores and his lies,
And I think: maybe you've never lived, studied, loved, and believed
(Because it's possible to make reality of all this without making anything
        of all this);
Maybe you've hardly existed, like a lizard with its tail cut off,
The tail squirming just short of the lizard.

I've made of myself what I haven't known,
And what I could have made of myself I didn't.
The masquerade I wore was wrong.
They believed the mask; I didn't contradict them, and lost myself.
When I wanted to take off the mask,
It was stuck to my face.
When I finally got it off and looked in the mirror,
I'd already aged.
I was drunk, I didn't know how to put on a mask I hadn't even taken off.
I threw away the mask and slept in the cloakroom
Like a dog tolerated by the management
For not making trouble
And I'm going to write it all down to prove I am sublime.

Musical essence of my useless verses,
If only I could encounter you as something I'd made,
And not remain always in front of the Tobacco Shop in front of me,
Crushing underfoot the awareness of existing and existing,
Like a rug a drunkard stumbles on,
Or a doormat the gypsies stole, even though it was worthless.

But the owner of the Tobacco Shop came to the door and stayed there.
I look at him with the discomfort of a misturned neck
And the discomfort of a misunderstanding soul.
He will die and I will die.
He'll leave his sign behind, I'll leave my verses.
At a certain point his sign will die, and my verses will die.
After that, the street where his sign was will die,

And the language in which I had written my verses.
Then the turning planet, where all of this took place, will die.
On other satellites in other systems something like people
Will continue making things like verses and living under things like signs,
Always one thing across from the other,
Always one thing just as useless as the other,
Always the impossible just as stupid as the real,
Always the mystery of the depths just as certain as the dream of the
          mystery of the surface,
Always this thing or that thing or neither one thing nor another.

But a man went into the Tobacco Shop (to buy tobacco?),
And plausible reality suddenly falls on top of me.
I start up energetic, convinced, human,
And plan to write these lines wherein I say the contrary.

I light a cigarette while thinking about writing them
And the cigarette tastes like liberation from all thought.
I follow the smoke like a path all its own,
And enjoy, in a moment both sensitive and competent,
The freeing of all my speculations
And the awareness that metaphysics is a consequence of being cranky.

Then I sit back in the chair
And continue smoking.
While Destiny grants it me, I'll continue to smoke.

(Maybe I'd be happy
If I married my washerwoman's daughter.)
That sinks in. I get out of the chair. I go to the window.

The man came out of the Tobacco Shop (stuffing change into his pants
          pocket?).
Hey, I know him: it's Esteves, who is without metaphysics.
(The Owner of the Tobacco Shop came to the door.)
As if by divine instinct, Esteves turned and saw me.
He waved goodbye, I shouted *So long, Esteves!*, and the universe

Reconstructed itself to me with neither ideal nor hope, and the Owner
of the Tobacco Shop smiled.

Lisbon, January 15, 1928

(variant title: March of the Downfall)

§

Almost without wanting to (as if we knew!) great men rise out of
        common men
Sergeant to emperor by imperceptible transitions,
Accomplishment mixes
With the dream of accomplishment to come,
And the road rolls its quick, invisible degrees.
Oh, those who see the end from the very start!
Oh, those who aspire to climb the flight!
The conqueror of every empire was always an assistant book-keeper,
Every king's lover—even those already dead—, a pensive, caring mother,
If only I could see souls inside, like bodies outside.

Ah, desire, what a prisonhouse!
What a madhouse, the meaning of life!

(1928?)

Neighborhood Gazette

Babylon's Lloyd Georges left
No trail on history.
Briands of Assyria or Egypt,
Trotskys of some Greek
Or Roman colony gone by—
All dead names, even written.

Only foolish poets, madmen
Who made their own philosophies,
And judicious old geometrists
Have survived that anterior,
Miniscule darkness—
Even history's not history.

Oh great men of the Moment!
Oh great seething glories
Obscurity flees!
Take it all unthinking!
Pad your fame and bellies—
Tomorrow's for the madmen of today!

(1928)

(variant title: Futurist Gazetteer)

§

In the darkling idiot conflict
Between light and shopkeeper,
Let the following truth
Be lit, however lightly.

Shopkeepers are accustomed
To mark up 100 percent
And protest any surplus
Paltry in their purview.

They cry dark perdition
When their exalted betters
Fail to uphold correct
Cutpurse tradition.

Shopkeepers, issue forth!
Steal 200 percent—:
End the endless argument
Between Cosa Nostra and Camorra…

* * *

Written in a Book Abandoned in Travel

I've come from around Beja.
I'm going to the middle of Lisbon.
I'm bringing nothing and I'll find nothing.
I have the anticipated weariness of what I won't find,
And the melancholy I feel is neither in the past nor in the future.
I leave written in this book the emblem of my final design:
I was as the weeds and they never tore me out.

(25/i/1928)

Marginalia

Making good use of time!
But what is time that I could make use of it?
Making good use of time!
No day without a line...
Honest and superior work...
Work like Virgil's, like Milton's...
But it's so difficult to be honest and superior!
So unlikely to become a Milton or a Virgil!

Making good use of time!
Break the soul into precise pieces—not too big, not too small—
Build well-jointed cubes
To make accurate engravings on history
(And they're just as accurate underneath, where you can't see)...
Turning sensations into cardcastles, poor ink spent at night,
Laying out thoughts in domino patterns, like against like,
And the will in a difficult carom...
Images of games, solitary pastimes—
Images of life, images of lives, Image of Life...

Verbalism...
Yes, verbalism!
Making good use of time!
That there be no minute unexamined by consciousness...
That there be no factitious or indefinite action...
That no movement disagree with intention...
The soul's good manners...
Grace in persisting...

Making good use of time!
My heart's as weary as an absolute beggar.
My brain's all set to go like that package sitting in the corner...
My song (verbalism!) is what it is and it's pretty sad.
Making good use of time!
It's five minutes since I began to write.

Have I made good use of them or not?
If I don't know if I've made good use of them, what'll I know about
    other minutes?

(Passenger who rode so many times in the compartment
With me on the suburban train,
Did you work up an interest in me?
Did I make good use of time looking at you?
What was the rhythm of our stillness on the moving train?
What was the understanding we never reached?
What was the life in it? What was it in my life?)

Making good use of time!...
Ah, let me make good use of nothing!
Not time, not being, not memories of time or being!
Let me be a leaf on a tree, tickled by a breeze,
The mindless autonomous dust on a road,
The random rivulet running at rain's end,
Tracks on the road lasting till the next wheel comes,
A trudging drifter who stops in his tracks
And sways with the same movement as the earth's
And shudders with the same movement as the soul's
And falls, like the gods fall, on Destiny's floor.

(11/iv/1928)

Demogorgon

Street full of empty sunlight. Walled houses, people walking.
A fearful sadness chills me.
I foresee something happening behind the façades, in the movement.

No, no, not that!
Anything but knowing what the Mystery is!
Surface of the Universe, O Lowered Eyelids,
Don't ever raise yourselves!
The sight of Ultimate Truth couldn't be endured!

Let me live without knowing anything, and die without coming to know
        anything!
The reason for being, the reason for there being beings, for everything
        being,
Would bring on a madness greater than the spaces
Between souls, between stars.

No, no, not the truth! Leave me these houses and these people,
Just this, nothing else, houses and people…
What cold horrible breath touches my closed eyes?
I don't want to open them from living! O Truth, forget about me!

(12/iv/1928)

Procrastination

The day after tomorrow, yes, only the day after tomorrow...
Tomorrow I'll start thinking about the day after tomorrow,
Maybe I could do it then; but not today...
No, nothing today; today I can't.
The confused persistence of my objective subjectivity,
The sleep of my real life, intercalated,
Anticipated, infinite weariness—
I'm worlds too weary to catch a trolley—
That kind of soul...
                    Only the day after tomorrow...
Today I want to prepare,
I want to prepare myself for tomorrow, when I'll think about the next day...
That'd be decisive.
I've already got the plans sketched out, but no, today I'm not making any
          plans...
Tomorrow's the day for plans.
Tomorrow I'll sit down at my desk to conquer the world;
But I'll only conquer the world the day after tomorrow...
I feel like crying,
I suddenly feel like crying a lot, inside...
That's all you're getting today, it's a secret, I'm not talking.
Only the day after tomorrow...
When I was a kid the Sunday circus diverted me every week.
Today all that diverts me is the Sunday circus from all the weeks of my
          childhood...
The day after tomorrow I'll be someone else,
My life will triumph,
All my real qualities—intelligent, well-read, practical—
Will be gathered together in a public notice...
But the public notice will go up tomorrow...
Today I want to sleep, I'll make a fair copy tomorrow...
For today, what show will repeat my childhood to me?
Even if I buy tickets tomorrow,
The show would still really be the day after tomorrow...
Not before...

The day after tomorrow I'll have the public pose I will have practiced
      tomorrow.
The day after tomorrow I'll finally be what I could never be today.
Only the day after tomorrow…
I'm sleepy as a stray dog's chill.
I'm really sleepy.
Tomorrow I'll tell you everything, or the day after tomorrow…
Yes, maybe only the day after tomorrow…

By and b…
Yes, the old by and by…

(14/iv/1928)

§

Master, my dear master!
Heart of my body—intellectual and all!
Life of the origin of my inspiration!
Master, what's become of you in this form of life?

You didn't care if you—or anyone else—lived or died,
Soul abstract and visual to the bone,
Marvelous attention to the ever-multiple exterior world,
Refuge from yearning for all the old gods,
Human spirit of the maternal earth,
Flower riding the flood of subjective intelligence…

Master, my master!
In sensationist anxiety of all the felt days,
In the humdrum heartbreak of the mathematics of being,
I, slave to everything, like some dust in every wind,
I lift my hands to you who are far, so far from me!

My master and my guide!
Whom nothing wounded, nothing hurt, nothing disturbed,
Sure as the sun involuntarily making its day,
Natural as the day showing everything forth,
Master, my heart never learned your serenity.
My heart never learned anything.
My heart is nothing.
My heart is lost.

Master, I would have been like you only if I had been you.
How sad the great day when first I saw you!
Since then, everything's weariness in this subjectivized world,
Everything's struggle in this world where things are desired,
Everything's a lie in this world where things are thought,
Everything's another in this world where everything's felt.
Since then, I've been like a beggar left out in the dew
By the whole village's indifference.

Since then, I've been like torn-up weeds
Left sheaved in patterns ruined by the wind,
Since then, I've been me, yes, me, to my utter misfortune,
And, to my utter misfortune, I'm not me or anyone else at all.
But then why did you teach me to see clearly,
If you couldn't teach me how to have the soul to see that clarity of sight?
Why did you call me to the mountaintops,
If I, a child of lowland cities, didn't know how to breathe?
Why did you give me your soul if I didn't know what to do with it,
Like somebody loaded down with gold in the desert,
Or singing with a divine voice among ruins?
Why did you awaken me to sensation and the new soul,
If I'll never know how to feel; if my soul's the same as always?

It would've pleased uncanny God if I'd remained forever
The decadent poet, stupidly pretentious,
Who one day might have been able at least to amuse,
If the dreadful science of seeing hadn't arisen in him.
Why did you turn me into me?
If only you'd left me human!

Happy the journeyman,
With his ordinary daily task, just as easy as it is hard,
With his ordinary life,
For whom pleasure is pleasure and fun is fun,
Who sleeps to sleep,
Who eats to eat,
Who drinks to drink, and so he's happy.

The calm you had, you gave to me, and for me it was distress.
You freed me, but human destiny is to be a slave.
You woke me, but being human means being asleep.

(15/iv/1928)

§

Sometimes I meditate,
Sometimes I meditate, and I meditate more deeply, and even more deeply,
And the whole mystery of things seems like oil on the surface,
And the whole universe is an ocean of faces with open eyes on me.
Each thing—a streetlight on the corner, a stone, a tree,
Stares at me from an incomprehensible abyss,
And every god marches through my head, and every idea about the gods.
Ah, there being things!
Ah, there being beings!
Ah, there being a way for there being beings to be,
For there being there being,
For there being there being as being,
For there being...
Ah, existing, the abstract phenomenon—existing,
There being consciousness and reality,
Whatever that means...
How can I express the horror all this causes in me?
How can I say what it's like to feel like this?
What's the soul of there being being?

Ah, the awful mystery of the tiniest thing's existing is awful
Because it's the awful mystery of there being anything at all...
Because it's the awful mystery of there being...

(29/iv/1928)

On the Last Page of a New Anthology

So many good poets!
So many good poems!
They're really good and all alike,
With so much concurrency not one stays with you,
Or they endure by chance, posterity's lottery,
Gaining place by the Impresario's whim…
So many good poets!
What am I writing poems for?
When I write them they seem to me
What my sensation, with which I write them, seems to me—
The only big thing in the world—
The universe outside swells with my largess.
Afterwards, written, right there, readable…
Well, now … And in this anthology of minor poets?
So many good poets!
What is genius, finally; how do you distinguish
Genius, or good poets from bad?
I have no idea if you can really distinguish…
It's better to sleep…
I shut the anthology more weary of it than I am of the world…
Am I vulgar?…
So many good poets!
Holy God!…

(1/v/1928)

§

In terrible night, the natural substance of every night,
A night of insomnia, the natural substance of all my nights,
I remember, on watch in an incommodious drowse,
I remember what I did and what I could have done in life.
I remember, and an anguish
Spreads all through me like a bodily chill or a fright.
What's irreparable in my life—that's what the corpse is!
Could be other corpses are illusion.
Could be the dead are alive in another place.
Could be all my own past moments exist somewhere,
In the illusion of space and of time,
In the falsity of elapsation.

But what I wasn't, what I didn't do, what I didn't even dream;
What only today I see I should have done;
What only today I see clearly I should have been—
That's what's dead beyond all the Gods,
That—and today it's the best of me—is what not even the Gods make live…

If at a certain point
I'd gone left instead of right;
If at a certain moment
I'd said yes instead of no, or no instead of yes;
If, during a certain conversation,
I'd had the sentences I elaborate only now, half-asleep—
If all of it had been that way
I'd be other today, and maybe the whole universe
Would be drawn imperceptibly into being other, too.

But I didn't turn to the irreparably lost side,
I didn't turn, I didn't even think about turning, and I see it only now;
But I didn't say no or I didn't say yes, and only now I see what I didn't say
But all the sentences I didn't have for saying at that moment surge up in me,
Clear, inevitable, natural,
The conversation bought to a conclusive conclusion,

The subject utterly resolved...
But only now what never was nor will be back there, hurts me.

What I really failed has no hope at all,
In no metaphysical system at all.
Could be I can take what I dreamed to another world,
But could I take to another world the thing I forgot to dream?
Yes, dreams to be, that's what the corpse is.
I'm burying it in my heart forever, for all time, for all the universes,
On this night when I'm not sleeping, and the quiet surrounds me
Like a truth I have no share in,
And, outside, the moonlight is as invisible to me as the hope I don't have.

(11/v/1928)

Clouds

On a sad day, my heart sadder than the day…
Moral and civil obligations?
Complexity of duties, of consequences?
No, nothing,
Sad day, no will for anything…
Nothing.

Others travel (I've traveled, too), others are in the sun
(I've been in the sun, too, or supposed I was),
They all have a reason, or life, or synthesized ignorance,
Vanity, joy, and sociability,
And they emigrate to come back, or not to come back
In ships that simply transport them.
They don't feel the death in every departure,
The mystery in every arrival,
The horror in everything new…
They don't feel: that's why they're senators and bankers,
They dance and have jobs in commerce,
They go to all the theaters and know people there…
They don't feel: why should they feel?

Cattle festooned in corrals of the Gods,
Let them go garlanded to sacrifice
Under the sun, sprightly, living, content to feel themselves so…
Let them go, but oh, I go with them
Ungarlanded to the same destiny!
I go with them without the sun I feel, without the life I have,
I go with them without their ignorance…

On a sad day, my heart sadder than the day
On a sad day, every day…
On such a sad day…

(13/v/1928)

§

At the wheel of a Chevrolet on the road to Sintra,
Through moonlight and dreams, on the deserted road,
I drive alone, drive almost slowly, and it almost
Seems to me, or I almost force myself to think it seems,
That I'm going down another road, another dream, another world,
That I'm going on without having left Lisbon, with no Sintra to go to,
That I'm going on, and what is there to going on but not stopping, but
      going on?

I'll spend the night in Sintra because I can't spend it in Lisbon,
But, when I get to Sintra, I'll be sorry I didn't stay in Lisbon.
Always this groundless worry, no purpose, no consequence,
Always, always, always,
This excessive anguish over nothing at all,
On the road to Sintra, on the road to dreams, on the road to life…

Alert to my subconscious movements at the wheel,
Around me, with me, leaps the car I borrowed.
I smile at the symbol, at thinking of it, at turning right.
In how many borrowed things do I move through the world?
How many borrowed things do I drive as if they were mine?
How many borrowed things—oh God—am I myself?

To my left, a hovel—yes, a hovel—by the roadside.
To my right an open field, the moon far off.
The car, which just now seemed to give me freedom,
Is now something I'm shut up in,
That I can only drive shut up in,
That I can only tame if I include it, if it includes me.

To my left, back there, that modest, that more than modest hovel.
Life must be happy there: it's not mine.
If someone saw me from the window, they'd think: Now, that guy's happy.

Maybe a child spying at the upstairs window
Would see me, in my borrowed car, as a dream, a fairy tale come true.
Maybe, for the girl who watched me, hearing my motor out the kitchen
        window,
On packed earth,
I'm some kind of prince of girls' hearts,
And she'll watch me sideways, out the window, past this curve where I
        lose myself.

Will I leave dreams behind me? Will the car?
I, the borrowed-car-driver, or the borrowed car I drive?

On the road to Sintra in moonlight, in sadness, before the fields and night,
Forlornly driving the borrowed Chevrolet,
I lose myself on the future road, I disappear in the distance I reach
And in a terrible, sudden, violent, inconceivable desire
I speed up,
But my heart stayed back on a pile of rocks I veered from, seeing without
        seeing it,
At the door of the hovel—
My empty heart,
My dissatisfied heart,
My heart more human than me, more exact than life.

On the road to Sintra, near midnight, in moonlight, at the wheel,
On the road to Sintra, oh my weary imagination,
On the road to Sintra, ever nearer to Sintra,
On the road to Sintra, ever farther from me…

(11/v/1928)

Nocturnal by Day

…No, what I have is my sleepiness.
What's that? Such weariness caused by responsibilities,
Such sorrow caused by maybe not being celebrated,
Such development of opinions on immortality…
What I have is my sleepiness, old friend, sleepiness…
Let me at least have that; who knows what else I'll ever have?

(16/vi/1928)

The Times

He sat down drunk at the table and wrote an editorial
For *The Times*, clear, unclassifiable, legible…,
Supposing (poor guy!) he could influence the world…

....

Dear God … Maybe he could!?

(16/viii/1928)

Song in the English Style

I cut relations with the sun and stars, wrote a full stop on the planet.
I brought everything I've known forever, wrapped in a little packet.
I traveled, buying useless things and discovering uncertainty,
And my heart's the same as it's always been—the desert and the sky.
I failed in what I was, in what I wanted, in what I know.
No darkness can steal, no light can wake me: I have no more soul.
I'm nothing but nausea, nothing but brooding, nothing at all but yearning,
I'm something far away from myself, out there in space, turning,
Simply because my being's much more comfortable than my not,
Stuck to one of the world's wheels, like a gob of snot.

(1/xii/1928)

§

Not a minute too soon … this is perfect…
There it is!
There's my madness, right there in my head!

My heart exploded like a cardboard bomb
And sent shockwaves up my spine right into my brain…

Thank God I'm nuts!
Thank God everything I ever did came back to me as trash,
Like I was spitting in the wind,
And spattered all over my face!
That everything I ever was got tangled underfoot
Like excelsior for shipping precisely nothing!
That everything I ever thought is sticking its finger down my throat
And making me want to puke on an empty stomach!
Thank God, because, like being drunk,
This is a solution.
How do you like that … I found a solution, but I had to use my stomach!
I found a truth, I felt it in my guts!

Transcendental poetry—already done it!
Grand lyric rapture—strictly old hat!
Organizing various poems by decreasing vastness of subject—
No news at all.
I need to throw up, to throw up my self…
I'm so nauseated that if I could eat the universe just to spew it into the
        sink, I'd do it.
It'd be a struggle, but there'd be a purpose to it.
At least there'd be a purpose.
The way things are, I don't have a purpose, or even a life.

* * *

§

The sly glance of the stupid worker at the crazy engineer—
The loopy engineer no longer engineering...
The smile I feel shared behind my back when I'm among the normals—
(When they look me in the face, I don't feel them smiling).

(22/i/1929)

Notation

My heart broke like an empty vase.
It fell outrageously downstairs.
A careless maid dropped it.
It fell and shattered into more pieces than there was china in the vase.

Asinine? Impossible? How should I know?
I have more feelings than I did when I felt like me.
I'm a scatter of shards, a glitter on the rug.

When it fell it made a noise like a breaking vase.
What gods there are lean over the banister,
Staring at the splinters their maid made of me.

They're not angry at her.
They forgive her.
What was I but a broken vase?

They look at the absurdly conscious shards—
Conscious of themselves, they're conscious of them—
They look and they smile.
They're smiling forgivingly at their harmless maid.

Scattered on the great stairway strewn with stars.
A bright shard, turned away from the lustrous exterior, among heavenly
        bodies.
My work? My one and only soul? My life?
A shard.
And the gods are watching it closely because they don't know what it's
        doing there.

* * *

§

Maybe I'm nothing more than my dream...
That smile will be for another, or for an intended other,
Frail blonde...
Her glance my way, casual as a calendar...
Her thanking me when I keep her from falling off the trolley,
A thanking...
Perfectly...
I love dreaming about what never came after
Our conversation, it never happened,
Some people never reach adulthood without [...]!
Actually, I think few people reach adulthood—few—
And those who do, just die and never notice a thing.

Frail blonde, figure of an Englishwoman absolutely Portuguese,
Every time I run into you I remember the lines I forgot...
Of course you don't mean a thing to me,
And I only remember forgetting you when I see you,
But running into you sums up the day and gives negligence
A surface poetry,
Something plus in the minus of life's futility.
Frail blonde, happy because you're not entirely real
Because nothing worth the trouble of remembering is entirely real,
And nothing worth the trouble of being real is really worth the trouble.

(25/i/1929)

43

Insomnia

I can't sleep, and I don't expect to sleep—
I don't even hope to sleep—not even in death.

Insomnia vast as the stars awaits me,
And a world-wide, useless yawn.

I can't sleep; I can't read when I lie awake at night,
I can't write when I lie awake at night,
I can't think when I lie awake at night—
My God, I can't even dream when I lie awake at night!

Ah, the opium of being any other person!

I can't sleep, here I lie, a corpse awake, feeling,
And my feeling is an empty thought.
They rush through my head in a jumble, things that happened to me—
I regret them, and blame myself—
They rush through my head in a jumble, things that didn't happen to me—
I regret them, and blame myself—
They rush through my head in a jumble, things without meaning—
I even regret and blame myself for them, and I can't sleep.
I don't have the strength to find the energy to light a cigarette.
I stare at my bedroom wall as if it were the Universe.
Outside, there's the silence of this whole thing.
A great appalling silence at any other time,
At any other time when I might be able to feel.

I'm writing really nice poems—
Poems saying I have nothing to say,
Poems insisting on saying it,
Poems, poems, poems, poems, poems...
So many poems...
And all truth, all life outside of them and me!

I'm tired, I can't sleep, I'm feeling, and I don't know what to feel about it.
I'm a sensation without a corresponding person,
An abstraction of self-consciousness with nothing inside
Except what's necessary to feel the consciousness,
Except—I have no idea except what!

I can't sleep. I can't sleep. I can't sleep.
Vast sleepiness throughout body and mind, covering my eyes, all through
       my soul!
The only thing not sleeping is my inability to sleep!

O daybreak, you're so late... Come...
Come, uselessly,
Bring me a day just like today, and a night just like tonight...
Come bring me the happiness of this sad hope,
Because you always bring happiness and hope,
According to the old literature of the senses.
Come, bring hope, come, bring hope.
My exhaustion sinks into my mattress.
My back hurts because I'm not lying on my side.
If I were lying on my side, my back would hurt from lying on my side.
Come on, daybreak, come!

What time is it? I don't know.
I don't have the energy to reach for the clock,
I don't have the energy for anything, not even for nothing...
Only for these lines, written the day after.
That's right, the day after.
Poems are always written the day after.

Absolute night, absolute quiet, outside.
All Nature at peace.
Humanity rests to forget its sorrow.
Exactly.
Humanity forgets its joys and sorrows.
That's what they say.

Humanity forgets, yes, humanity forgets,
But even awake, Humanity forgets.
Exactly. But I can't sleep.

(27/iii/1929)

Chance

By chance, in the street, the blonde girl, by chance.
But no, she's not that one.

The other was on another street, in another city, and I was another...

Suddenly, I lose my immediate vision,
I'm in the other city again, on the other street,
And the other girl goes by.

What great advantage accrues to such intransigent recollection!
Now I feel sorry because I never saw the other girl again
And I feel sorry in the end because I never even looked at this one.

It really helps to have an inside-out soul!
At least poems get written.
Poems get written, you're taken for a nut, and then for a genius, maybe,
If it fits, or even if it doesn't fit,
Celebrity, how wonderful!

I was saying at least poems get written...
This one was about a girl,
About a blonde girl,
But what about her?
There was one I saw a long time ago in another city,
On another kind of street;
And there was the one I saw a long time ago in another city,
On another kind of street;
Because all recollections are the same recollection,
Everything past is the same death,
Yesterday, today, maybe even tomorrow, who knows?

A passerby looks at me with occasional estrangement.
Was I making a poem out of grimace and gesticulation?
Could be ... and the blonde girl?

Well, she's the same one, in the end...
It's all the same, in the end...

Except, I'm not the same in some way, which is the same old thing, anyway.

(27/iii/1929)

§

Ah, open another reality to me!
I want to be like Blake, visited by angels:
I want to have visions for breakfast.
I want to meet fairies in the street!
I want to imagine myself out of this jerry-rigged world,
This cobbled-together civilization.
I want to live like a banner in the breeze,
Some symbol of something fluttering over something else!

Then bury me wherever you want.
My true heart will go on keeping watch—
Sphinx-emblazoned sail—
Atop the mast of visions
In Mystery's four winds.
North—what everyone needs
South—what everyone desires
East—where everything comes from
West—where everything ends
—The four winds of civilization's mystic air
—The four ways of unreason, and of learning the world

(4/iv/1929)

Marinetti, Academician

Here they all come, here comes everybody...
Any day, unless there's a sale on, I'll arrive, too...
Everyone was born for this...

I can't get out of it except by dying beforehand,
I can't get out of it except by climbing the Great Wall...
If I stay here, they'll socialize me...

Here comes everybody, because they were born to This,
And you only arrive at it by being born to it...

Here comes everybody...
Marinetti, academic...

The Muses will avenge themselves with electric lamps, old friend,
In the end they'll set you up in footlights in an old cellar,
And your dynamic, always a bit Italian, f-f-f-f-f-f.........

(7/iv/1929)

§

My heart, mystery flogged by sails in the wind...
Flag snaps unfurled on high,
Tree kneaded, bent, shaken by the gale,
Agitated, green froth stuck on,
[...]
Sentenced forever to the root of all unutterability!
I wanted to say it out loud with a voice to really say it!
I wanted to bring at least one other heart a knowledge of mine!
I wanted to put myself out there...
But what am I? Tatter once flag,
Fallen leaves blown aside,
Words misunderstood socially even by their appreciators,
What I wanted was my whole soul,
But it was only a beggar's hat under a car,
Ruined ruins,
And laughter from the express is loud back there on the road of happy
        people...

(10/v/1929)

Quasi

Straighten up, build shelves for will and action…
I want to do it now, like I always do, with the same result;
But it feels so good to have clear intentions—firm in clarity only—to do
      something!

I'm going to pack my bags for the Definitive,
Organize Álvaro de Campos,
And tomorrow I'll be the same thing as the day before yesterday—that
      proparoxytone eternity.

I'm smiling in anticipated knowledge of the non-thing I'll be…
Well, at least I'm smiling; smiling's always something…

Romantic products, all of us…
If we weren't products of romanticism, we wouldn't be anything…

That's how you make literature…
Poor little Gods, that's how you make life!

Others are romantic, too,
Others don't realize anything, either, and they're rich and poor,
Spend their lives looking at bags to pack,
Sleep next to half-composed papers,
Others are me, too.

Pushcart lady singing an unconscious hymn to your wares,
Cog in the economy's clock shop,
Present and future mother of the dead in the hulling of Empires,
Your voice comes to me like a call to nowhere, like the silence of life…

I look up from the papers I'm thinking of not putting in order after all
To the window where I didn't see the pushcart lady I heard through it,
And my smile, which still hasn't left me, dies in my mental metaphysics.
Sitting at my desk, I refused to believe in all the gods and my desk is still
      a mess,

I faced every fate head on because I was distracted by a peddler calling
      outside,
And my weariness is an old boat rotting on a deserted beach.
With that image from any old poet, I shut the desk and my poem.

Like a god, I never straightened anything out, not my life, not the truth.

(15/v/1929)

§

To have no duties, no set hours, not even realities…
To be a human bird
In haleyonic flight over the world's intransigence—
Earning my nightly bread by the sweat of someone else's brow—
Sad jack-of-all-trades
In a colosseum full of tears, age-old compère,
A little more full than the Venus de Milo, even,
In the insubsistence of all contingencies.
And a little sun, at least, for the dreams where I don't live.

* * *

§

Ah, to flake out, how utterly refreshing!
It's just like being in the country!
What a relief to be totally untrustworthy!
I'm breathing easier, now that the time for the appointment is over.
I flaked on them, deliberately derelict,
Kept waiting for the urge to go out and I knew it would never come.
I'm free, contra organized, clothed society.
I'm naked. I dive into the waters of my imagination.
It's too late to get to any of the places I should have been at the same time,
Deliberately at the same time…
It's OK, I'll stay home dreaming poems and smiling in italics.
What fun to simply watch as life goes by!
I can't even bring myself to light the next cigarette … If it's an act,
Let it stay with all the others waiting for me in the broken dates of life.

(17/vi/1929)

Poem of the Song About Hope

I.

Give me lilies, lilies,
And roses too.
But if you have no lilies
Or roses to give me,
At least have the desire
To give me lilies
And roses too.
The desire's enough,
Your desire, if you have it,
To give me lilies
And roses too,
And I'll have lilies—
The best lilies—
And the best roses
Without receiving anything
Except the gift
Of your desire
To give me lilies
And roses too.

II.

The dress you're wearing
Is a memory
For my heart.
Someone else wore it long ago—
I never saw her,
But I remember.
Everything in life
Works through memory.
Some woman moves us
With a gesture and we remember our mother.
Some girl makes us happy

When she talks just like our sister.
A child tears us from distraction
Because we loved a woman like her
When we were young, and never spoke to her.
Everything's like that, more or less.
The heart jolts along.
Living means not meeting up with yourself.
At the end of it all, if I'm tired, I'll sleep.
But I'd like to meet you
And I'd like for us to speak.
I'm sure we'd get along well, you and I.
But if we don't meet, I'll hold on to the moment
When I thought we might.
I keep everything—
All the letters I've been written,
All the letters I've never been written,
Oh for Christ's sake, people keep everything whether they want to or not,
And your little blue dress? my God, if only I could use it
To pull you close!
Well, anything can happen…
You're so young—so full of youth, Ricardo Reis would say—
And my vision of you explodes literarily,
And I lie back on the sand and laugh like a low-grade elemental.
Damn, feeling wears you right out, and life is warm when the sun is high.
Good night in Australia!

* * *

§

I know already: someone told the truth…
Even the clotheslines look worried.
Objectivity comes in for a visit,
And we stay outside, sheets on a line
Caught in the rain, forgotten in a street where all the windows are shut.

* * *

§

Don't worry about me; I have the truth, too.
I've got it coming out of my pockets like an illusionist.
I belong, too…
No one gets done without me, naturally,
And being sad is having ideas about these things.
O my capers on aristocratic terraces,
You eat porridge in shirtsleeves in my heart.

(18/vi/1929)

§

Ah, in the terrible silence of my bedroom,
The clock with its sound made of silence!
Monotony!
Won't someone give me back my lost childhood?
Won't somebody help me find it in the middle of God's road—
It's utterly lost, like a hanky on the train.

(16/viii/1929)

§

And I who am drunk on all the world's injustice...
—God's flood and the little blonde baby floating on the water,
I, in whose heart the anguish of others is rage,
And that vast humiliation, the existence of a taciturn love—
I, the lyricist who makes sentences because I couldn't make my luck,
I, the ghost of my redeeming desire, cold fog—
I don't know if I should make poems, write words, because the soul—
The innumerable soul of others suffers forever outside me.

My verses are my impotence.
What I can't do, I write;
And the different rhythms I write alleviate my cowardice.

The gullible seamstress seduced and violated,
The apprentice rat caught forever by the tail,
The prosperous businessman enslaved by his prosperity
—I don't distinguish, I don't praise, I don't [...]—
They're all human animals, suffering stupidly.

Feeling all this, thinking all this, raving all this,
I break my heart portentously, like a mirror,
And all the world's injustice is cardiac in me.

My coffin heart, my [...] heart, my gibbet heart—
All crimes are committed and paid for inside me.

Teary eyes, how useless, humanity's neurological mush,
Drunk on altruistic servility,
Voice in curlers, crying in the wilderness fourth floor left...

* * *

Diluent

The lady in number 14 laughed today, at the door
Where just a month ago, her little son left in a coffin.
She laughed naturally, with her soul all over her face.
One thing's for sure, and that's life.
Sorrow doesn't last because sorrow doesn't last.
That's for sure.
I repeat: for sure.
But my heart isn't sure.
My romantic heart makes riddles out of life's egoism.

Here's the lesson, oh soul of people!
If the mother forgets the son who left her when he died,
Who's going to do the work it'll take to remember me?
I'm alone in the world like a top about to topple.
I can die like dew dries.
Through a natural art of solar nature,
I can die at the will of forgetfulness,
I can die like nobody else...
But this hurts,
This is indecent for someone who has a heart...
This...
Yes, it sticks in my craw like a sandwich over-stuffed with tears...
Glory? Love? The yearning of a human soul?
Inside-out apotheosis...
Give me Vidago Water*—, I want to forget about life!

(29/viii/1929)

* Obvious pun aside, Vidago is a parish in Southern Portugal; *
it is famous for its mineral water.

§

Oh hell I know it's only natural,
But you gotta have a heart!…
Goodnight and shit!
(Crack, my heart!)
(Shit for all humanity!)

In the house of the mother whose son was run over,
Everybody's laughing, everybody's having a great time.
There's all this noise of horns and nobody remembers

They got their compensation:
Baby = X!
They're enjoying X right now.
They're eating and drinking the dead baby.
Bravo! That's people for you!
Bravo! That's humanity!
Bravo! Brava! That's all fathers and mothers
With babies waiting to be run over!
Money makes you forget.
Baby = X.

You could wallpaper a house.
You could pay the last installment on the furniture.
Poor little baby.
But if he hadn't been run over, what would our bills be?
Yes, we loved him so.
Yes, he was so dear to us
And then he died.
Life goes on. He died!
It's such a pity. He died!
But he left what you pay bills with
And that's something.
(Of course, it was a disaster.)
But the bills got paid.
(And, of course, that poor little boy

Got smashed to a pulp)
But now at least we don't owe the grocer.
(Yes, it's a shame, but there's always a good side to things.)

Baby died, but what survived is ten thousand cruzeiros.
Yeah, ten grand.
You can do a lot (poor baby!) with ten grand.
You can pay your debts (dear little baby)
With ten grand.
Make things right
(Pretty little boy who died) with ten grand.
Ten grand.
Oh, you know it's so sad
(Ten grand).
A kid of ours got run over
(Ten grand),
But when you think about remodeling the house
(Ten grand),
Renovating the den
(Ten grand),
Well, that makes you forget (we're crying and crying!)
(Ten grand!), doesn't it?
It must have been God's will
(Ten grand).
Poor slaughtered baby!
Ten grand.

* * *

De la musique...

Ah, little by little, among the ancient trees,
Her figure comes forth and I stop thinking...

Little by little, I come forth, from my own anguish...

Two figures meet in a lakeside clearing...

...Two dreamed figures,
For this was all moonlight and one of my sadnesses,
And a supposition of something else,
And the result of existing...

Really, did two figures meet
In a lakeside clearing?
        (... What if they don't exist?)

...In a lakeside clearing.....................

(17/ix/1929)

Ka-Pow!

Today, since I really don't know what to say, and don't much care—
Intelligent, sure, but bored stiff with most things everywhere—,
I'll write my epitaph: Álvaro de Campos, here lies me
(The rest of it is in the Greek Anthology)...
But hey, what the hell's going on with all this rhyming?
Well, I ran into this friend of mine named Simon
Who asked what I've been up to all this time and
This poem's just because I had so little to tell
The guy... I'd never rhyme—most poets can't do it well—,
But sometimes it's what you need and that's the perfect hell
Of it. Just now, my heart popped like a blown-up paper bag
Against the wall and startled some suit I never met in the act
Of going by. He turned and looked kind of hard at me,
So I'm ending this poem indeterminately.

(2/xii/1929)

§

Never, no matter how much I travel, how much I know
What it means to leave a place, to arrive at a place, known or unknown,
I lose, at departing, at arriving and on the moving line between them,
The shivering sensation, the fear of the new, the nausea—
Nausea, the sensation of knowing the body has a soul.
Thirty days of travel, three days of travel, three hours of travel—
Oppression oozes deep into my soul.

(31/xii/1929—Évora)

§

I go by on a suburban street in the evening.
I'm coming back from a conference full of adepts like me.
I return alone, a poet again, unskilled, without engineering,
Human down to the sound of my solitary shoes in the onset of night
While in the distance the door of the last open shop is covered by the last
        shutter.
Ah, the sound of dinner in happy households!
I go by. My ears see inside the houses.
My natural exile is moved to compassion in the darkness
Of the street my hearth, the street my being, the street my blood.
O to be the economically guaranteed kid,
With the fluffy bed and the sleep of children and a nanny!
O my underprivileged heart!
My excluded sensibility!
O my heart broken so excessively by me being me!

Who used my little cradle for firewood?
Who washed the floor with rags made from my little sheets?
Who tossed the little white smock I wore when they baptized me
On top of the rinds and household lint in the trashcans of the world?
Who sold me into Destiny?
Who gave me me for change?

I come from speaking precisely, in positive circumstances.
I made concrete points, like a numbering machine.
I was balanced as a scale.
I said it like I knew it.

Now, on the trolley line from the terminus whence one returns to the city,
I go by, a metaphysical bandit by the light of staggered lamp-posts,
And in the shadow between them, I want so much to go no farther.
But I caught the trolley.
The little bell rings twice at the invisible end of the cord pulled
By the thick-fingered hands of the conductor. He needs a shave.
I caught the trolley.

Oh, man... in spite of everything, I caught the trolley—
Always, always, always...
I always go back to the city,
I always go back to the city after speculations and detours,
I always go back wanting to eat dinner.
But I never sat to the kind of dinner I hear through the venetian blinds
On happy houses in the outskirts where you come back on the trolley,
The conjugal houses of life's normality!
I pay the fare through the bars and the conductor
Looks right through me as if I were the *Critique of Pure Reason*...
I paid the fare. I did what's right. I'm just an ordinary guy, after all.
There's no cure for any of this, not even suicide.

(6/i/1930)

§

Today, since I'm lacking everything, as if I were the floor,
Since I know myself atrociously, since all the literature
I use for myself, to own consciousness of myself,
Fell, like the paper wrapping on a crappy bon-bon—
Today my soul looks just like nerve-death—
Necrosis of the soul,
Rotting of the senses.
However much I've done, I see clearly: it's nothing.
However much I dreamed, could have been dreamed by the porter.
However much I loved, if today I can remember what I did love, died
        long ago.
O Paradise Lost of my bourgeois childhood,
O Eden, my nighttime tea cozy,
My crocheted bedspread when I was a boy!
Destiny finished with me like an interrupted manuscript.
Neither high nor low—consciousness of not even having it…
The old spinster's curlers—my whole life.
I have a stomach ache in my lungs.
It costs me plenty to breathe enough to keep up a soul.
I have an array of sad diseases in the joints of my will.
My poet's garland—you were paper flowers,
Your presumed immortality was the life you didn't possess.
My poet's laurel crown—petrarchically dreamed,
Capeless, but with some fame,
No dice, but with God—
Counterfeit wine list in the last corner tavern!

(9/iii/1930)

§

There are so many gods!
They're like books—no one can read them all, you never know anything.
People who only know one god and keep it secret—how happy they
        must be.
Every day I believe something different—
Sometimes I believe different things on the same day—
And I'd love to be the kid who's down there now,
Crossing my view through the open window—
Eating a cheap little cake (she's poor) with neither apparent nor final cause,
Useless animal raised above other vertebrates
And singing, between her teeth, an obscene song from a musical revue…
Yes, there are a lot of gods…
But I gave everything to the god who led that kid away…

(9/iii/1930)

§

Cesário,* who succeeded
In seeing clearly, simply, purely,
In seeing the world in its things,
In being a gaze with a soul behind it and so short a life!
Lisboetan** child of the Universe,
Bless you and all you see!
My heart festoons Praça da Figueira in your honor
And there's no corner not looking at you in all the corners of your corners.

(6/iv/1930)

---

* *Cesário Verde (1855–1886), great Baudelairean poet of Lisbon.*
** Alfacinha, *"Little Lettuce", nickname for Lisboetans.*

Carry Nation

Not an aesthetical saint like Teresa,
Not a dogmatic saint,
Not a saint.
But a human saint, mad and divine,
Maternal, aggressively maternal,
Hateful, like all saints,
Persistent, with sanctity's madness.
I hate her and my hat's off
And I'm shouting viva her and have no idea why!
North American stupor—a starry aureole!
Well-meaning witch...
Don't pluck wild roses!
Amidst laurels, laurels of exaltation
We raise you to glory and insult!
To the health of your immortality
We drink a strong drunkard's wine.

I, who never did a thing in the world,
I, who never knew how to want or how to know,
I, who was always the absence of my will,
I salute you, mad little mother, sentimental system!
Paradigm of human aspiration!
Marvel of the good deed, of a great will!

My Joan of Arc without a motherland!
My human Saint Teresa!
Stupid like all saints,
Militant as a soul's wish to conquer the world!

You should be saluted with the wine you abhorred!
We canonize you with shouted weeping toasts!

We salute you, enemy to enemy!
I, so often falling-down drunk just because I didn't want to feel,
I, so often inebriated because I don't have enough of a soul,

I, your contrary,
I raise my sword to the angels, Eden's guardian angels,
And I raise it in ecstasy,
And I shout your name.

(8/iv/1930)

§

Something unmemorious comes through the foggy day.
Softly with the evening comes opportunity for loss.
I go to sleep unsleeping in the open air of life.

It's useless telling me actions have consequences.
It's useless knowing actions use consequences.
It's all useless, it's all useless, it's all useless.

Through the foggy day comes absolutely nothing.

I just had this real live impulse
To go wait for someone coming in on the train from Europe,
To go to the docks and watch the ships come in and feel sorry for
        everything.

With the evening comes no opportunity at all.

(21/iv/1930)

At the Trolley Stop

Bring me platters loaded with forgetting!
I want to wolf down the abandonment of life!
I want to break this habit of screaming inside.
Enough, damn it! I don't know what of, but by now I've had enough…
So, live tomorrow, huh?… And what do you do about today?
Live tomorrow because you've put off today?
Did you buy a ticket to the show without noticing?
Anyone capable of laughter would just explode, imagine the guffaws!
And now the trolley comes—the one I was waiting for—
Another came before… And I have to get on now!
Nobody's making me, but why let it go by?
Just let them all go by, and me, and life…
My conscious soul is such an ache in my real stomach!
What a good sleep it'd be to be any other person…
Now I understand why all kids want to be a brakeman…
No, I don't understand anything…
Afternoon all blue and gold, people's happiness, life's bright eyes…

(28/v/1930)

Birthday

In the days when they used to celebrate my birthday,
I was happy and no one was dead.
In my old house, even my birthday was tradition for centuries,
And everyone's happiness, even mine, was upheld like a religion.

In the days when they used to celebrate my birthday,
I had the health that comes from not seeing anything at all,
From being knowledgeable only within my family,
And from not having the hopes the others had for me.
When I came to have hopes, I no longer knew how to have hopes.
When I came to look at life, I'd lost the sense of life.

Yes, what I was by my own supposing,
What I was by heart and parentage,
What those long evenings in the provinces made me,
What them loving me and me being their boy made me,
What I was—oh, my God!, until today, I didn't know what I was...
So distant!...
(Not even an echo...)
The days when they used to celebrate my birthday!

What I am today is dampness in the back hall,
Making things sprout on the walls...
What I am today (and the house of those who loved me shimmers
        through my tears),
What I am today is they've sold the house,
And all of them are dead.
What I am today is outliving myself like a spent match...

In the days when they used to celebrate my birthday...
That love of mine was like a person, those days!
Physical desire of the soul to meet itself there another time,
On a voyage both metaphysical and fleshly,
With the duality of I and me,...
Wolfing the past like bread, without time like butter in your teeth!

I see everything again so clearly it blinds me to what's right here...
There's the table set with more places than usual, more of our best
china, more cups,
The over-loaded side-board—sweets, fruit, more in shadow under the
shelf—,
My old aunts, all my different cousins, and everything for my sake,
In the days when they used to celebrate my birthday...

Stop, my heart!
Don't think! Leave thinking to the brain!
O my God, my God, my God!
Today I don't have birthdays.
I last.
The days add themselves to me.
I'll be old when I get there.
Nothing else.
Damn me for not keeping the past purloined in my pocket!

The days when they used to celebrate my birthday!

October 15, 1929*

(13/vi/1930)

* *Campos' birthday.*

§

I'm tired of intelligence.
Thinking wreaks havoc on the emotions.
There are horrible side-effects.

You suddenly weep, and all your dead aunts start making tea again
In your old house with its older yard.
Stop, my heart!
Silence, factitious hope!
If only I were nothing but the boy I was…
I slept well because I was simply tired and had no ideas to forget!
My horizon was the yard, the beach,
And my end before my beginning!

I'm tired of intelligence.
If at least I could perceive something with it!
But all I perceive is weariness deep
As hovering lees aswirl in goblets,
Those things wine has to give it body.

(8/vi/1930)

Diagnostic

So little truth! So little truth!
I'm OK when I'm not thinking.
So little truth…
Slowly…
Someone could come to the window…
Nothing to do with emotions!
Careful!
Yes, if I could just accept it…
You wouldn't have to insist, I'd accept it…
What for?
What a question! I'd just accept it…

(18/vi/1930)

Bicarbonate of Soda

Sudden anguish…
Ah, such anguish, such nausea, stomach to soul!
What friends I've had! All the cities I've been through, what voids!
What metaphysical dung, all my designs!

An anguish,
A disconsolation of the soul's epidermis,
A falling of arms at the sunset of struggle…
I deny it.
I deny everything.
I deny more than everything.
I deny with arms and ends all the Gods and their negation.

But what's this I feel missing in my stomach, in the circulation of my blood?
What empty swoon wears out my brain?

Should I have a drink or commit suicide?
No: I'm going to exist. Damn! I'm going to exist.
To ex-ist…
To ex ist…

My God… Buddhism, chill my blood!
To renounce all landscapes with the doors
Wide open before the landscape,
Hopeless, in liberty,
Without nexus,
Accident of the inconsequential surface of things,
Monotonous but sleepy,
And such breezes when all the doors and windows are open!
What an agreeable summer for others!

Give me something to drink—I'm not even thirsty!

(20/vi/1930)

§

That English girl, so blonde, so young, so nice,
Who wanted to marry me...
What a pity I didn't marry her...
I would've been happy,
But how do I know I would've been happy?
How do I know what could have been
About what might have been, if it's what never was?

Today I regret I never married her,
But before even the hypothesis of my having been able to marry her.
And so it's all regret,
And regret is pure abstraction.
It gives you a certain discomfort
But it also gives you a certain dream...

Yes, that girl was one of the opportunities of my soul.
Today the regret is what's withdrawn from my soul.
Holy God! What complications from not marrying an Englishwoman
          who must have forgotten me by now!...
But what if she hasn't forgotten me?
(These things do happen.) What if she still remembers me and she's constant
(Sorry if you think I'm ugly, but ugly men are loved, too,
Even sometimes by women!)?
If she didn't forget me, she still remembers me.
This is really already another kind of regret,
And there's no forgetting it, when you make someone suffer.

But, in the end, these are all vanity's conjectures.
It'd be nice if she remembered me, with her fourth kid in her arms,
Leaning over the *Daily Mirror* to look at Princess Mary.

At least it's better to think it's that way.
It's a picture of a suburban English house,
A good inner landscape of blonde hair,
And regrets are the shadows...

In any case, if it's like that, there's a hint of jealousy left.
The fourth kid with another man, the *Daily Mirror* in their house.
What could have been…
They're eating marmalade at tea time in England…
I wreak vengeance on the whole English bourgeoisie by being a fool of a
        Portuguese.

Ah, but still I see
A gaze really as sincere as the blue
Looking like another kid at me…
And it's not with poetry's salty jokes I erase you from the image
Of you in my heart;
I'm not disguising you, my only love, and I don't want anything from life.

(29/vi/1930)

Cul de Lampe

Little by little,
Without missing anything,
Without anything left me,
Without anything exactly in the same position,
I go on walking standing still,
I go on living dying,
I go on being me through a mass of beingless people.
I go on being everything but me.
I finished.

Little by little
Without anyone telling me
(What does what I've been told in my life matter?)
Without anyone listening to me
(What does what I've said or what you heard I said matter?)
Without anyone wanting me...
(What does what someone said when they told me what they wanted
        matter?),
OK...
Little by little,
Without any of this,
Without anything that's not this,
I'll go on,
I'll stop,
I finished.

What ended!?
I'm fed up with feeling and pretending to think,
And I'm still not finished.
I still am writing poems.
I still am writing.
I still am.

(No, I'm not going to finish
Yet...

I'm not going to finish.
I finished.)

Suddenly on a side street, a high window and what's that shape in it,
And the horror of having lost the childhood where I wasn't,
And the vagabond way of my unworkable consciousness.

What more do you want? I finished!
Neither lacking the neighbor's canary, O morning of another time,
Nor the full-basket sound of the baker in the stairwell,
Nor the I don't know where I am anymore proclamations,
Nor the funeral (I hear their voices) in the street,
Nor the sudden thunder of wooden shutters in the summer air,
Nor... so many things, so many souls, so few fixable!
Finally, now, everything cocaines along...
My childhood love!
My bygone bib!
My peaceful bread, the good butter by the window!
Enough, now I'm blind to what I see!
God damn it, I'm finished!
Enough!

(2/vii/1930)

§

Well, yes, of course,
The Universe is black, especially at night.
But I'm like everybody,
I have toothaches or bunions and those aches pass.
You make poems with the other aches.
The ones that hurt make you cry out.

The inner constitution of poetry
Helps a lot…
(Like analgesic works for soulaches—they're mild…)
Let me sleep.

(3/vii/1930)

§

For all that, for all that,
There were also swords and colored pennants
In the springtime of what I dreamed for myself.
And hope, too,
Bedewed the fields of my involuntary vision,
And I had someone smiling back at me, too.

Today, I'm as if I'd been another.
I don't remember who I was, except as an appended history.
Who I'll be interests me just about as much
As I care about the future of the world.

Suddenly, I fell down the stairs,
And the sound of the fall was the fall's guffaw.
Each step was an importune, iron testament
To the ridiculous display I made of myself.

Poor guy who didn't get the job for lack of a clean overcoat to wear when
        he showed up,
But the rich and noble guy who lost
Love's position because he wasn't wearing a good overcoat in his desire,
        poor him, too.
I'm impartial as the snow.
I never preferred poor to rich,
Just like I never preferred anything to anything in me.

I always saw the world independently of me.
And behind it, my very living sensations,
But that was another world.
For all that, my heartbreak never made me look at orange and see black.
The external world above everything!
And me, putting up with myself and with whatever's with me.

* * *

§

I'd love to love to love.
Just a second… hand me a cigarette
From the pack on top of the night-stand.
Go on… You were saying
That something got lost
In the development of metaphysics
Between Kant and Hegel.
I agree, absolutely.
I was really listening.
Nondum amabam et amare amabam (Saint Augustine).
What a curious thing, these associations of ideas!
I'm worn out from thinking about feeling something else.
Thanks. Let me light up. Go on. Hegel…

* * *

§

My poor friend, I don't have any compassion to give you.
Compassion's costly, especially when it's sincere, and on a rainy day.
I mean, there's a price to be paid for feeling on a rainy day.
So let's feel the rain and leave psychology to another kind of sky.

So, it's a sexual preoccupation?
But when you're older than fifteen that's indecent.
Preoccupation with the, let us say, opposite sex and its psychology,
But this is stupid, sonnyboy.
The opposite sex exists to be chased after, not understood.
The problem exists to be resolved, not to be worried about.
Understanding makes you impotent.
And you shouldn't reveal so much of yourself.
"La Colère de Samson," do you know it?
"La femme, enfant malade et [...]"
But it's not like that at all.
Stop making me feel sorry for you, it's so boring!
Look: it's all literature.
It comes to us from outside, like the rain.
In a way we're pages of novels come to life—
Translations, sonnyboy.

You know why it's so sad? It's because of Plato,
Who you never read.
Your Italian sonnet (you never read Petrarch) came out all wrong,
And that's just the way life is.

Roll up the sleeves of your civilized shirt
And dig in exact soils!
That's worth more than bothering with someone else's soul.

We're nothing but the ghosts of ghosts,
And the landscape isn't helping much today.
It's all geographically outer.
The rain falls because of natural law
And humanity loves because it's been told about love...

(9/vii/1930)

§

Life is for the unconscious (O Lydia, Célimène, Daisy)
And the conscious are for the dead—the conscious without Life…
I smoke a cigarette; it smells like other people's heartbreak,
And for them I'm ridiculous because I observe them and they observe me.
But I couldn't care less.
I unfold into Caeiro and technique
—Machine technician, people technician, fashion technician—
And I'm in no way responsible for what I find around me, not even in
        poetry.
The tattered silk-sewn standard of the Maple empires?*—
Go ahead. Shove it in the drawer where you keep
All that posthumous junk of yours and get it over with.

* *Obscure.*

* * *

§

I sold myself for nothing to random acquaintance.
I loved where I found it, a little by forgetting.
I was leaping from interval to interval,
And thus I arrived where I arrived in life.

Today, remembering the past,
I don't find anything in it except who I wasn't…
The unconscious kid in the house now ended,
The bigger kid wandering in the house of his aunt now dead,
The unconscious teenager in the care of the priest cousin he treated
        like an uncle,
The bigger teenager sent abroad (new tutor's mania).
The unconscious young man studying in Scotland,
The unconscious young man now a man fed up with studying in Scotland.
And then the unconscious man, so diverse and so stupid…
Nothing in common with what I was,
Nothing the same as what I think,
Nothing in common with what I could have been.
I…

I sold myself for nothing and got beans for change—
Beans from the table games of my swept-out childhood.

(19/vii/1930)

§

No! All I want is freedom!
Love, glory, money—they're prisons.
High-class rooms? Swanky furniture? Cushy rugs?

Ah, but let me leave so I can go meet myself.
I want to breathe the air all alone,
I don't have a lockstep pulse,
I have no quota to make for society,
I'm not anything but me, I wasn't born anything but who I am, I'm full
    of me.
Where do I want to sleep? In the back yard…
No walls at all—a great understanding—
Me and the Universe,
And that quiet, that peace, before sleep, seeing not the ghost in the closet
But the great splendor, black and fresh, all the stars at once,
And the great infinite abyss on high
Sends down healthy breezes across the skull-stretched flesh of my face,
Where only my eyes—another sky—reveal the great subjective being.

I don't want it! Give me freedom!
I want to be equal to myself.
Don't geld me with ideas!
Don't make me dress up in the straightjacket of manners!
Don't make me eulogizable or intelligible!
Don't kill me in life!

I want to know how to throw that ball at the moon
And hear it fall in the back yard!
I want to go lie down on the lawn, thinking "tomorrow I'll look for it"…
Tomorrow I'll go look for it in the back yard…
Tomorrow I'll go look for it in the back yard…
Tomorrow I'll go look for it in the yard
Look for it in the yard…
In the back
Yard…

(11/viii/1930)

§

Freedom, yes freedom!
True freedom!
To think without desire or conviction,
To be one's own master without the influence of novels!
To exist without Freud or airplanes,
Without cabarets, not even in the soul, without velocities, not even in
        weariness!
The freedom of wandering, of sane thought, of love of natural things,
The freedom to love the morals you need to give to life!
Like the moon when the clouds break,
The great Christian freedom of my once-prayerful childhood
Suddenly extends over the whole earth its cloak of silver for me…
Freedom, lucidity, coherent reason,
The juridical notion of the souls of others as human,
The joy of having those things, a being able once again
To enjoy the fields without referring to anything
And drink water as if it were all the wines in the world!

Steps all baby-steps…
Old woman's goodly smile…
Hold the hand of my earnest friend…
What a life mine has been!
How much time waiting at the flag stop!
How much living printed on the flyers of life!

Ah, I have a healthy thirst. Give me freedom,
Give it to me in the old ladle by the jug
In the country house of my old childhood…
I drank and it gurgled,
I was fresh and it was fresh,
And, as there was nothing to harass me, I was free.
So, what's become of the ladle and innocence?
What's become of the one I should have been?
And except for all this desire for freedom and good and air, what's become
        of me?

(17/viii/1930)

§

Great are the deserts, and everything is desert.
A few tons of rock with bricks on top
Won't disguise the ground, the very ground all is.
Great are the deserts, and souls are deserted and great—
Deserted because they're crossed only by themselves,
Great because from there you see everything, and everything's dead.

Great are the deserts, my soul!
Great are the deserts.

I never got a ticket for life.
I picked the wrong door for feeling.
There wasn't a wish or a chance I didn't lose.
Today there's nothing left for me, the night before the trip,
With my open suitcase still waiting to be packed,
As I sit on the chair with the pile of shirts that won't fit in,
Today there's nothing left (aside from the discomfort of sitting here)
But knowing this:
Great are the deserts, and everything is desert.
Great is life, and life's not worth the trouble.

I'll pack the suitcase better with an eye toward thinking of packing
Than I would by packing it with my fake hands (I've made myself clear,
        right?).
I light a cigarette to put off the trip,
To put off all trips,
To put off the whole universe.

Come back tomorrow, reality!
That's enough for today, folks!
Come back later, absolute present!
It's better not to have to be like this.

Buy chocolates for the child I replaced by mistake,
And take off the wrapper, because tomorrow is forever.

But I have to pack the suitcase,
I definitely have to pack the suitcase,
The suitcase.
I can't take my shirts in a hypothesis and my suitcase in reason.
Yes, all my life I've needed to pack the suitcase.
But also, all my life, I've been sitting in the corner on a pile of shirts,
Chewing—like a bull who never became Apis—destiny's cud.

I have to pack the suitcase of being.
I must exist packing suitcases.
My cigarette ash falls on the top shirt of the mountain.
I glance at it and verify: I am asleep.
All I know is I have to pack the suitcase,
And the deserts are great and everything is desert,
And some parable about all this, but I forgot it already.

Suddenly I rise like all Caesars.
Once and for all, I'm going to pack the suitcase.
Damn it, I'll pack it and close it;
I'll watch them take it out of here;
I'll exist independently of it.

Great are the deserts and everything is desert—
Unless, of course, I'm mistaken.

Poor human soul with the only oasis in the desert next door!

Better pack the suitcase.
The end.

(9/iv/1930)

§

That same old *Tuecro duce e auspice Teucro*
It's always *cras*—tomorrow—we'll go to sea.

Soft, useless heart!
Soft, there's nothing to hope for,
So there's no need to despair…
Soft… Over the back yard wall
Someone else's olive grove rises in the distance.
I saw one as a kid and it wasn't that one:
I don't know if the same eyes or the same soul saw it.
We put everything off, till death comes.
We put everything off and the understanding of everything,
With a foreseen weariness of everything,
With a prognostical, empty *saudade*.

* * *

Tatter

The day came down raining.
This morning the sky was pretty blue, though.
The day came down raining.
I've been a little blue all day.
Anticipation? sadness? neither?
I don't know; I woke up feeling sad, that's all.
The day came down raining.

I know overcast days are elegant.
I know the sun oppresses elegant people because it's so ordinary.
I know that being susceptible to changing light isn't elegant.
But who's telling the sun and everything else I want to be elegant?
They gave me the blue sky and a sun I can see,
Mist, rain, shades of gray—I've got those things inside me.
All I want today is peace and quiet.
I'd even love a hearth, as long as I didn't have one!
I've gotten sleepy from wanting peace and quiet.
Let's not exaggerate!
I am, in fact, sleepy—I don't have to explain myself.
The day came down raining.

Caring? Affection? They're memories…
Only kids have them…
My lost dawn, my only real blue sky!
The day came down raining.

The housekeeper's daughter's beautiful mouth…
Pulp of a heart's fruit for eating…
When was that? I don't know…
This morning, when the sky was blue…

The day came down raining.

(10/ix/1930)

§

I'm starting to get to know myself. I don't exist.
I'm the interval between what I desire to be and what others made me,
Or half the interval, anyway, because there's life, too…
Well, that's about it, that's me all over…
Turn off the light, close the door, quit the sound of slippers in the hall.
Stay alone in my room with the peace and quiet of my very own self.
What a crappy universe.

* * *

§

I've written more poems than you could believe.
I've written mostly
Because others have written.
If there were never poets in the world,
Would I be capable of being the first?
Never!
I'd be a perfectly permissible individual,
With morals and my own house.
Oh, Senhora Gertrudes!
You missed a few spots
When you cleaned my room...
Get these ideas out of here!

(15/x/1930)

§

The placid anonymous face of a dead man.

Thus the ancient Portuguese mariners
Sailored on though they feared the great ocean of the End
And finally saw neither monsters nor the abyss,
But marvelous beaches and stars yet unseen.

What do the world's metal shutters hide in the shop windows of God?

* * *

§

I have a miserable cold,
And everybody knows how miserable colds
Change the whole system of the universe,
Make you angry at life—
You even sneeze metaphysics.
I've wasted the day blowing my nose.
I have a fuzzy headache.
Sad condition for a minor poet!
Today I truly am a minor poet.
Once upon a time I was a desire; it came undone.

Farewell forever, fairy-queen!
You had sunlight wings and here I am walking.
I won't get well unless I lie down in bed.
I've never been well except when I've been lying down on the universe.
Excusez du peu... My God, I'm so blocked!
I need truth and aspirin.

(14/iii/1931)

Oxfordshire

I want what's best, I want what's worst, but really I want nothing at all.
I'm uncomfortable lying on my right side, uncomfortable on my left,
And uncomfortable lying on my conscious existence.
I'm universally uncomfortable, metaphysically uncomfortable,
But the hell of it is I've got a headache.
That's more serious than the meaning of the Universe.

Once, near Oxford, on a walk in the countryside,
From the curve in a road, I saw, in the near distance,
A steeple rise above village houses.
I have a photographic recall of that null event,
Like a tranverse fold wrecks the crease in your trousers,
And here comes the punchline...
From the road I saw age-old spirituality
In that steeple, and assiduous charity.
From the town, when I got there, the steeple was a steeple,
But most of all, it was there.

You'd be happy in Australia, as long as you didn't have to go.

(4/vi/1931)

§

Yes, I'm me, myself, just as I've resulted from everything,
A kind of accessory, my own spare part,
Irregular environs of my sincere emotion,
I'm I, here in me, I'm me.

Whatever I was, whatever I wasn't, all that's me.
Whatever I wanted, whatever I didn't want, all that formed me.
Whatever I loved or stopped loving, it's the same yearning in me.

And, at the same time, the impression, a little inconsequential,
Like a dream formed out of mixed realities,
Of having left myself, to myself, on a trolley bench,
To be found by chance when someone comes along and sits on it.

And, at the same time, a little distant,
Like a dream you'd want to remember in the penumbra you wake up to,
Of there being better than me in me.

Yes, at the same time, the impression, a little painful,
Of waking into a day full of creditors,
Of having failed everything like you trip over a doormat,
Of having wrapped everything up like in a trunk you haven't brushed out,
Of having substituted something for my self somewhere in life.

Enough! The impression is one—more or less metaphysical,
Like the last sun in the window of a house you're leaving—
Of it being worth more to be a child than to want to understand the world,
The impression of bread and butter and toys,
Of a great quiet having nothing to do with the Gardens of Proserpine,
Of good will toward life leaning its forehead on the window
With the sound of rain outside,
Not the grown-up tears so hard to swallow.

Enough, yes, enough! I'm I, myself, the trade-in,
The emissary with neither card nor credential,

The unsmiling clown, the fool in someone else's oversized suit,
With a tinkling in his head
Like little bells ringing the servants upstairs.

I'm myself, the syncopated charade
No one can figure out at a party in the provinces.

I'm myself, what a relief!

(6/viii/1931)

Ah, a Sonnet...

As for my heart, it's an insane admiral
Who abandoned his profession of the sea
And lives to reminisce, little by little,
Pacing at home, forever pacing away...

In the movement (I transport myself
Into this chair just by imagining)
The long-abandoned sea maintains its focus
In muscles worn out from so much constant halting.

Saudade inhabits the bones of my arms and legs.
There are saudades coursing through my brain
And my colossal rages made all of fatigue...

But—hey, this is good!—the conversation
Was about my heart ... and what the hell am I doing
With the admiral instead of my sensation?

12/x/1931

(variant title: Sonnet, to Seem Normal)

§

My heart, the mistaken admiral,
Commanded an armada to be,
Essayed the passage Fate denied him,
Wished to be happy—, more fool he.

Land-locked, absurd, disregarded
—The results of his own self-avoidance—,
Nothing happened, nothing happened, nothing happened,
As these broken lines show him at a glance.

But there is absolving recompense and sweet
In the shadows—the silence of the rout
Holds more soul's roses than victory.

And so embarked an Imperial Fleet
Charged with yearning, charged with glory,
To accompany the admiral on his route.

* * *

§

Lately, I've been writing regular sonnets
(Well, nearly regular) just like any old poet, I swear!...
But if I told someone of the full sorrow
Makes me do such things (and put on such airs),

They would hardly believe it. O great seas
Of emotion vanishing into blackest mist
Till heartbreak is the heartbreak of an ascete.
[…]

Like the snap-to of a pressure spring
I shut the pages of my appointment book
Wherein I fix congenital indecision;

I am neither my being, nor my thinking;
My life, a prince on a balcony […]
[…]

* * *

§

Don't talk so loud, this here is life—
Life and consciousness of it,
Because the night goes on, I'm tired, I'm not sleeping,
And, if I end up at the window,
I see, from under idiot eyelids, the many places of the stars...
I wore out the day with hopes of sleeping at night,
It's night now, almost another day. I'm sleepy. I'm not sleeping.
I feel I'm all humanity through my tiredness—
This tiredness almost turns my bones into froth...
That's what we all are...
We jitter like flies, our wings caught up
In the world, that spider web over the abyss.

(21/x/1931)

§

OK, I'm not right...
Allow me to distract myself from mental argument,
I'm not right, OK, it's being right just like any other way...

Do I even believe?
I believe I do. But I'm repeating myself.
Should love be constant?
Yes, love should be constant,
But only in love, of course.
I say it yet again...

What chaos people set up in their lives!
OK, all right, I'll bring the money tomorrow.

O great sun, you know nothing of this,
How happy you must be, unable to stare at the serene, unreachable blue.

(30/x/1931)

§

Useless to prolong the conversation about all this silence.
You sit slumped and smoking in the corner of the big sofa—
I sit slumped and smoking in the deep sofa-like armchair,
Nothing between us, going on an hour,
Except looks from a single impulse to say something.
We only refresh our cigarettes—the next lit on the ember of the last—
And continue the silent conversation interrupted
Only by the gazed wish to speak...

Yes, it's useless,
But everything, even life in the open air, is equally useless
And some things are hard to say...
This problem, for example.
Which one of us does she love? How can we start discussing this?
Not talk about her, don't you think?
And, above all, not to be the first to think about talking about her!
To talk about her to the impassive other, the friend...
Ash from your cigarette fell on your black jacket—
I was going to tell you, but then I'd have to talk...

We look at each other again like passing passersby.
And the mutual sin we didn't commit
Looms at once in the depth of two gazes.
Suddenly you stretch, half-rise—excuse your speaking...
"I'm going to bed!" you say to yourself, because you're going to say it.
And this whole thing, so psychological, so involuntary,
All because of an attractive, solemn woman who works at the office.
Ah, let's go to bed!
If poems are written about this, as you surely know, it's all for sneering!

(22/xi/1931)

110

§

I wake up at night, very much at night, in all silence.
The day—visible tick-tock—four hours late.
I open the window directly, in insomnia's despair.
And, suddenly, human,
The crossed square of a lit window!
Brotherhood by night!

Involuntary incognito brotherhood by night!
We're both awake and humanity is another.
It sleeps. We have light.

Who can you be? Are you sick, a counterfeiter, simply unsleeping, like me?
It doesn't matter. Eternal, unformed, infinite night
Only has, in this place, the humanity of our two windows,
The latent heart of our two lights,
In this moment and place, not knowing one another, we're all of life.
Over the windowsill on the back of the house,
Feeling the night-wet wood I clutch,
I lean out to the infinite and, a little, to me.

Not even roosters crowing yet in the definitive silence!
What are you doing, comrade of the lit window?
Dream, lack of sleep, life?
Full yellow tone of your unknown window…
It's funny: you don't have electric light.
Oh oil lamps of my lost childhood!

(25/xi/1931, a.m.)

Notes About Tavira

Here at last, in the town where I grew up.
I got off the bus, recollected myself, looked, saw, compared.
(It took all the time of a weary gaze).
Everything's old where it was new.
At once—other shops, other paintings on the fronts of the same old
        buildings—
A car I never saw (there weren't any then)
Stagnates dark yellow in front of a half-open door.
Everything's old where it was new.
Yes, because even things younger than me mean the rest is older.
The house they painted again is older because they painted it again.
I stop in front of the landscape, and what I see is me.
Back then, I saw myself splendid at 40—
Lord of the world—
41 and sluggish, I get off the bus.
What did I conquer? Nothing.
As a matter of fact, I really have conquered nothing.
I carry my boredom and my bankruptcy physically in my bag's
        increasing weight...
Suddenly I proceed surely, resolutely.
All hesitation gone.
This town of my childhood is a strange city, after all.
(I'm at ease, as ever, before the strange, which, to me, is nothing.)
I'm an outsider, a tourist, a passerby.
Of course: that's what I am.
Even in myself, for Christ's sake, even in myself.

(8/xii/1931)

§

I want to end among roses, since I loved them in childhood.
Chrysanthemums from later on, I plucked their petals in cold blood.
Speak little and slowly.
Don't let me hear you, especially in thought.
What did I want? My hands are empty,
Clenched mournfully on some far-off coverlet.
What did I think? My mouth is dry, abstract.
What did I live? It was so good to sleep!

(8/xii/1931)

§

No, it's not weariness…
It's a mass of disillusion
Stabbing me in some kind of thinking,
An inside-out Sunday
Of sentiment,
A weekend in the abyss…

No, it's not weariness…
It's me being existing,
And the world, too,
With everything both contain,
Everything folded up in there,
And, finally, it's the same variegated thing in duplicate.

No: weariness for what?
It's an abstract sensation
Of concrete life—
Something like a cry
For crying,
Something like an anguish
For anguishing,
Or for total suffering,
Or for suffering like…
Yes, for suffering like…
That's it, like…

Like what?
If I knew there wouldn't be this fake weariness in me.

(Ah, blind street-singers,
What a formidable hurdy-gurdy!
A man's gitarra, another's guitar, a woman's voice!)

Because I hear, I see.
I confess: it's weariness!…

§

The human soul is as filthy as an asshole
And the Advantages of Crookdom loom large in many imaginations.

It's all so nauseating—as if my heart were another stomach.
The Round Table was sold by weight,
And King Arthur's biography—a journalist wrote it...
But the Cavalry's scrap iron
Still reigns in our souls, like a distant profile

It's cold.
I put a cape over my shoulders—it reminds me of a shawl—
The shawl my aunt used to put over my shoulder when I was a kid.
But my childhood shoulders so disappeared inside my shoulders.
And my child's heart so disappeared inside my heart.

Yes, it's cold.
It's cold in everything I am, it's cold...
My very ideas are cold, like old folks...
And the chill I catch from my ideas being cold is even colder than them.

I wrinkle the cape around me...
The universe of people ... people ... every single person!
Multiplicity of blended humanity
Yes, what they call life, as if there were no other, or no stars...
Yes, life...

My shoulders droop so much, the cape slips down...
You want better commentary? Pull up my cape.

Ah, break the face of life and
Be free, roaring in your own quietude!

* * *

§

Moments of pleasure are few in life…
The thing to do is go for it… Yes, I've heard it said many a time
And I've even said it myself. (Repeating is living.)
The thing to do is go for it, don't you think?

Let's go for it, false blonde, go for it, casual and incognito,
You and your cinematographically distinct gestures,
Your sidelong looks at nothing,
Fulfilling your function as an animal ensnared,
Me on a plane of consciousness slanting toward indifference,
Let's love each other here. Time's only a day.
Let's hold on to all the romance!
I keep involuntary watch behind my back.
I'm something in the words I say to you, and they're smooth—and they're
        what you're waiting for
On this side of my Alps, and what Alps! we are of the body.
Nothing breaks the promised passage of a future connection,
And everything goes so elegantly, like in Paris, London, Berlin.
"I can see," you say, "that you've lived much abroad."
And I feel vanity when I hear it!
I'm just afraid you're going to tell me about your life…
A cabaret in Lisbon? Well, that's where we are, so OK.
Suddenly, I have a visual memory of a notice in the paper:
"High society rendezvous",
All that stuff.
But none of these foolhardy future reflections
Interrupt this conversation where I'm something to you.
I talk in halves and imitations
And each time, I see and feel, you like me more really than […] today;

At this point, leaning suddenly over the table,
I whisper a perfectly befitting secret.
You laugh, all look, part mouth, effusive and near,
And I really, really love you.
Resounds within us the sexual act of leaving.

I roll my head at the bill…
Happy, lively, feeling yourself, you talk…
I smile.
Behind the smile, I'm not me.

(5/ii/1932)

§

Ah, how extraordinary,
In our great moments of quiet sadness,
Like when someone dies and we're in their house all silent,
A car drives by in the street, or a rooster crows in a yard…
How far from life! It's another world.
We turn to the window, the sun shines outside—
Vast placid quietness of uninterrupted nature!

(28/iii/1932)

Costa do Sol

I

You can get all torn up by anything.
While blood and roses are in the world alive
There will always be certain good times
When things come to be, yet are not things.

My heart is a jolt, or rather, perhaps
A conscious interval. Cenotaphs rise
Over all those who like me suffered fits
Of going out to conquer the obstinate.

But the rocket is a symbol; it flies
To fall, after all its noise on high,
A mere senile tube, and even drops

On whoever lit it ... And what that street kid picks up—
Spent, hot tube—is just the thing I'm missing...
What absurd pyrotechnic lifts me up?

II

Gods, I leave behind the ancient Dame
(With a different letter do I fix
The absurd, and laugh, because I suffer). I say:
I leave behind the one I loved, like a prefix...

Olden I, anonymous and prolix
(Two adjectives I have followed all my days),
Loved for to have a heart-felt friend. Today
I love the thing I love because I hunt it.

Give me the wine a Horace sang!
I want to forget what of mine is mine...
I want to go forth without moving an inch.

I'm in Estoril and I watch the sky...
Ah, I'm so glad it's still there... that blue oval
Scattered stars over the Aegean sea.

III

We are the boys of a past springtime
Someone used to make those bricks. Pondering,
From my cigarette case I draw a mysticism
In light and smoke as if I'd forgotten.

In your air of sleeping in that chair
(I notice now, the exorcism done,
The third sonnet emerges from the abyss),
You are always the same—anonymous—third...

O great Atlantic ocean, I beg your pardon!
I who spat three sonnets at your shore,
Yes, but I spat them all on my own blame.

Woman, love, [alcove?]—you are tercets!
Only you, O sea and sky, you free us!
You shred any unknown rag to tatters...

....

Repose? Good old days? Goodbye, already!
Marília de Dirceu* was written in jail.
The only thing I really have is me.

If I could thwart that thing lying in wait
In me (in you, pale imperfect profile
Dead cut-out against a living sky...

(9/ix/1932)

* *Title of a very famous long poem by the Brazilian Arcadian,*
Tomás Antônio Gonzaga (1744–1810).

§

Ah, how the old days were different from what I didn't have!
How I loved when I loved. Ah, how I laughed.
As with eyes of one who never saw
I held the throne whereon to seat a queen.

While my life tramples me under my own feet
You lounge so utterly in evening chill...
O pierless, muckless, breezeless, odorless sea
What do you want with me? whose soul is mine?

As we sit under this low tea umbrella
Our oppository recollection comes so sudden...
My old yard and all the spreading branches

Above our little snack... Oh love, oh glory!
Shut my eyes to all of history!
Like frogs, we leap and jump right off the path...

* * *

Reality

Yes, I used to go by here all the time twenty years ago.
Nothing's changed in this part of the city—
Nothing I've noticed, anyway.

Twenty years ago!
What I was then! Somebody else...
Twenty years ago, and the houses don't know a thing...

Twenty useless years (but I have no idea if they were!
How do I know what's useful or not?)...
Twenty lost years (but what would it mean if I got them back?)

I'm trying to use my imagination to reconstruct
What I was and what I was like when I went by
Twenty years ago...
I don't remember, I can't remember.
The other one who went by here back then,
If he were around today, maybe he'd remember...
There are so many characters in novels who know their insides better
Than that me-myself who went by here twenty years ago!

Yes, the mystery of time.
Yes, the not knowing anything,
Yes, we all of us having been born on board.
Yes, yes, all that, or another way of saying it...

From that second floor window, still the same as itself,
Leaned out a girl older than me, so very memorable in blue.
If it happened today, what would that be?
We can imagine everything we know nothing about.
I'm physically and morally stuck: I don't want to imagine anything...

There was a day when I walked up this street thinking happily of the future,
Since God let what doesn't exist be all lit up.
Walking down this street today, I'm not thinking happily about the past.

At most, I don't even think…
I have the impression that the two figures are passing in the streets, neither
        then nor now
But right here, no time to disrupt the passing.
We'll look at each other indifferently.
Old me keeps walking up the street imagining a sunflower future.
Modern me keeps walking down the street imagining nothing.

Maybe this is really happening…
Really happening…
Yes, flesh and blood happening…

Yes, maybe…

(15/xii/1932)

§

And the splendor of maps, abstract road to concrete imagination,
Letters and random strokes open into wonder.

What dreaming in dusty bindings
And signatures, so complex (or so simple and graceful), of old books.
(Distant, discolored ink, here beyond death,
Time's visible enigma, the living nothing we are!)
What we forget daily, comes back in drawings,
What certain engraved announcements accidentally announce.

Everything suggests or expresses what it doesn't express,
Everything says what it doesn't say,
And the soul dreams on, different, distracted.

(14/i/1933)

§

In my old aunts' big living room
The clock ticked the time more slowly.
Ah, the horror of the happiness you didn't know
Because you knew it without knowing it,
The horror of what was because what is, is here.
Tea and biscuits in the provincial bygone,
In so many cities you've been my memory and tears!
Eternally a child,
Eternally left behind,
Since the tea and the toast went missing in my heart.

Heat up, my heart!
Heat up in the past,
The present is only a street where passersby just forgot me...

(29/i/1933)

§

The false, rigid clarity, non-home of hospitals
The human joy, living, over the lady next door's,
The inconsolable mother whose son died last year.

We make rags, we love rags, we are rags—
It's all rags in this world!

(29/i/1933)

In the MS, there is a line between the stanzas, which may mean that this is two separate texts.

§

Ah, the swipe of the washerwoman's iron
At the side window and my childhood leans out!
The sound of clothes washed in a tub!
All these things are, in some way,
Part of what I am.
(O dead maid, what about your grayheaded care?)
My childhood as tall as my face poking over the table…
My fat little hand on the tablecloth with the winding embroidery.
I looked across the settings, on tiptoe.
(Today when I stand on tiptoe, it's only intellectually.)
And the table I have, there's no tablecloth, and no one around to put
        one on…
I've studied bankruptcy's ferment
In the demonology of imagination…

* * *

§

Accentuated sound only in the clock
In the night with nobody else in houses at provincial dinnertime,
Sets all time on top of my soul;
While my old aunt's teatime doesn't come,
My heart hears time pass and suffers with me.

Ticking more somnolent than other clocks'—
This wooden one on the wall has a pendulum and it sways.
My heart misses something, who knows what.
I have to die…
Mechanical, serene ticking—serene, mechanical overtime in the provinces…

* * *

§

Fog of all memories together
(Blond schoolteacher in a peaceful playground)
I remember golden sun and silky paper...
A kid's hoop goes by so fast it almost knocks me down...

* * *

§

O night serene!
O pale moonlight!
O little boat dancing
On the sea at night!

Suavely, the past—the one here, Lisbon—arrives in me:
Third floor full of aunts, the peace back then,
All kinds of peace,
Childhood, no future dreamt,
Apparently endless noise of their sewing machine,
And everything fine and on time
With a fineness and on-time-ness long dead.

My God, what did I do with my life?

O night serene!
O pale moonlight!
O little boat dancing
On the sea at night!

Who used to sing that?
It was right there.
I remember but I forget
And it hurts, it hurts, it hurts…

For the love of God, stop the noise in my head.

* * *

§

I'm thinking about you in the silence of the night, when everything is
     nothing,
And the noises in silence are the silence itself,
And then, all alone, by myself, a passenger halted
On a voyage in God, uselessly, I'm thinking about you.

All the past, in which you were an eternal moment,
Is like this silence made of everything.
Everything lost, of which you were what I lost most,
Is like these noises.
Everything useless, among which you were someone not to be,
Is like the nothing to be in this night silence.

I've seen—or heard about—the death
Of so many I loved or knew,
I've seen—knowing nothing else about them—so many who were
With me, person or conversation, it doesn't matter much,
Or a people erased from the world,
And today the world for me is a cemetery at night,
Black and white, gravestones and trees in someone else's moonlight,
And this absurd restfulness… all through myself and everything else,
     I'm thinking about you.

(written on an envelope postmarked 15/iii/1933)

§

Pack your bags for Nowhere At All!
Embark upon the negative universality of everything
With a grand bedecking of make-believe ships—
Childhood's little, multicolor ships!
Pack your bags for the Grand Abandon!
And don't forget, with your brushes and scissors,
The polychrome distance of what you can't get.
Pack your bags definitively!
Who are you here, where you exist, gregarious and useless—
The more useful, the more useless—
The more true, the more false—
Who are you here? Who are you here? Who are you here?
Embark, even without any bags, on your own diverse self!
What's the inhabited earth to you, except what's not with you?

(2/v/1933)

Psychotype

Symbols. Everything, symbols...
Oh, yeah? Everything's a symbol...
Are you a symbol, too?

In exile from you, I look at your white hands
Resting (good English manners) on the tablecloth,
Persons independent of you...
I look at them: Are they symbols, too?
So, is the whole world symbol and magic?
Well, maybe so...
And why not?

Symbols...
I'm tired of thinking...
I finally raise my eyes to your eyes as they eye me.
You smile, knowing full well what I was thinking about...
My God! and you don't know...
I was thinking about symbols...
I respond faithfully to your conversation on top of the table...
"It was very strange, wasn't it?"
"Awfully strange. And how did it end?"
"Well, it didn't end. It never does, you know."
Yes, *you know* ... I know...
Yes, I know...
That's the bad thing about symbols, *you know.*
Yes, I know.
Perfectly natural conversation ... But symbols?
I can't take my eyes off your hands ... What are they?
My God! Symbols ... Symbols...

(7/xi/1933)

Italicized words are in English in the original.

Magnificat

When will this internal night, the universe, pass,
And I, my soul, have my day?
When will I awake from being awake?
I don't know. The high bright sun,
Impossible to stare at.
Cold blinking of stars,
Impossible to count.
Alien pulsing heart,
Impossible to hear.
When will it end, this theaterless drama,
This dramaless theater,
And I return to my home?
Where? How? When?
Cat fixing me with eyes of life,
Who do you hold in their depths?
It is He! It is he!
He who like Joshua will order the sun stand still and I will awake.
Then it will be day.
Smile, sleeping soul!
Laugh, my soul, it will be day!

(7/xi/1933)

Original Sin

Ah, who will write the history
Of whatever might have been?
If someone wrote it, that would be
The true history of humanity.

All there really is is the world, it's not us, only the world,
What there's not is us, and the truth's in there.

I'm someone who failed to be.
We're all what we suppose ourselves.
Our reality is the one thing we'll never manage.

What is that truth of ours—the dream of childhood's window?
What is that certainty of ours—the proposal on later's table?

I'm meditating, head bowed against superimposed hands
On the high ledge of the balcony window,
Sitting on the edge of a chair, after dinner.

What's my reality's, if all I have is life?
What's mine, if all I am is the someone I exist?

I've been so many Caesars!

In soul, and with some truth,
In imagination, and with some justice,
In intelligence, and with some right—
My God! my God! my God!—
I've been so many Caesars!
I've been so many Caesars!
I've been so many Caesars!

World, December 7, 1933

Typing

All alone in my engineer's cubicle, I sketch out a few plans,
I shape a project, isolated here,
Remote even from who I am.

Beside me, creepily banal accompaniment,
The cracking tic-tac of the typewriters.

What nausea of life!
What abjection, this regularity!
What a sleep, this being like this!

Back then, when I was someone else, there were castles and cavalries
(Illustrations, perhaps, from any children's book),
Back then, when I was true to my dream,
There were great passages in the North, explicit with snow,
There were great palm groves in the South, opulent with greens.

Back then...

Beside me, creepily banal accompaniment,
The cracking tic-tac of the typewriters.

We all have two lives:
The true one we dream in childhood
And continue to dream as adults in a misty substrate;
The false one we live among others,
The practical life, the useful life—
It ends up sticking us in a coffin.

In the other, there are no coffins, no deaths.
There are only illustrations of childhood:
Big colorful books to look at, not to read;
Big pages full of colors to remember later.
In the other, we're us,
In the other, we live;

In this one, we die: the meaning of life.
In this moment, in this nausea, I only live in the other...

But, to the side, creepily banal accompaniment,
Acting up rudely, raising its voice, I awake to
The cracking tic-tac of the typewriters.

(19/xii/1933)

§

To have no feelings, desires, impulses,
But to be, in the sensual air of things,
Nothing but an abstract emotion with wings of thought,

Not to be dishonest, not to be not dishonest, separate or conjoined,
Not the same as others, not different from others,
To live them in another, to separate from them
The way one, distracted, is forgotten by one's own self…

* * *

§

Wouldn't it be better
Not to do anything?
To drop everything and go pell-mell down through life
To a waterless shipwreck?

Wouldn't it be better
Not to pick anything
Off the rosebush in your dreams,
And lie quiet, thinking of the exile of others,
In springtimes to be?

Wouldn't it be better
To renounce, like the bursting of toy balloons
In an atmosphere of open markets,
Everything,
Yes, everything,
Absolutely everything?

(12/iv/1934)

§

They stuck a lid on me—
The whole sky.
They stuck a lid on me.

Such grand aspirations!
Such mighty plenitude!
Even a few truths…
But they stuck a lid
On all of it.
Like one of those old chamberpots—
Out there in the backwaters of tradition—
A lid.

(12/iv/1934)

§

Lisbon with its houses
Of many colors,
Lisbon with its houses
Of many colors,
Lisbon with its houses
Of many colors...
So different, it can only be monotonous,
Just like, from feeling so much, I can only think.

If, at night, lying awake
In the useless lucidity of sleeplessness,
I want to imagine one thing,
And another comes up (because I'm sleepy,
And where there's sleep, there's always a little bit of dream),
I want to see farther into the vista I glimpse
Through great fantastic palms,
But all I see
Against some kind of screen inside my eyelids,
Is Lisbon with its houses
Of many colors.

I smile, because, here, stretched out, it's something else.
It's so monotonous, it can only appear different.
And I'm so much me, I can only sleep and forget I exist.

All that's left, without me who I forgot because I'm asleep,
Is Lisbon with its houses
Of many colors.

(11/v/1934)

§

This old anguish,
This anguish I've held for centuries in me,
Overflowed its vessel
In tears, in grand imaginations,
In dreams the style of terrorless nightmares,
In great sudden senseless emotions.

Overflowed.
How will I ever get through life
With this unease putting creases in my soul?
If I'd at least gone truly mad!
But no: it's this being in between,
This almost,
This being able to be...
This.

Someone committed to an asylum is at least someone.
I'm committed to an asylum without an asylum.
I'm clear and crazy,
I'm coldly insane,
I'm apart from everything and equal to all:
I'm in a waking sleep dreaming dreams
Insane because they're not dreams.
That's how it is with me...

Poor old house of my lost childhood!
Who's there to tell you I've become so unprotected?
What's become of your boy? He's gone mad.
What's become of the one sleeping softly under your provincial ceiling?
He's gone mad.
Whose who was I? He's gone mad. Today he's who I am.

If I at least had religion, any religion!
If I believed, for example, in that fetish
I had in that house, in that one brought from Africa.

It was the ugliest thing, it was grotesque,
But it had the divinity of everything believed in.
If only I could believe in a fetish—
Jupiter, Jehovah, Humanity—
Any at all would do for me,
Because what is everything, besides what we think of it?

Crack, heart of painted glass!

(16/vi/1934)

§

In the house in front of me and my dreams,
There's always so much happiness!

I don't know the people who live there. I've seen, but never saw them.
They're happy because I'm not.

The kids who play on high balconies
Live among vases of flowers,
Eternally, no doubt.

Voices rise out of the interior of the domestic.
They always sing, no doubt.
Yes, they must sing.

Over there, when there's a party outside, there's a party inside.
It has to be that way where everything is well-adjusted—
Humans to Nature, because the city is Nature.

What great happiness, not being me!

But don't the others feel this way, too?
What others? There are no others.
What the others feel is a house with a closed window,
Or, when it's open,
It's for the kids to play on the porch, behind the wooden bars
Among the vase of flowers I never saw what kind they were.

The others never feel.
The ones who feel are us.
Yes, all of us,
Even me, who, at this moment, feel nothing.

Nothing? I don't know...
This nothing hurts...

(16/vi/1934)

144

§

I got off the train,
Said goodbye to my traveling companion,
We'd been together for eighteen hours.
The agreeable conversation,
The brotherhood of travel,
I felt sorry to get off the train, to leave him.
Casual friend whose name I never knew.
My eyes, I felt them billow a tide of tears...
Every leave-taking is a death...
Yes, every leave-taking is a death.
When we're on the train called life,
We're all casual with one another,
And we all feel sorry when we finally get off.

Everything human moves me, because I'm human.
Everything moves me because I have
Not some semblance of ideas or doctrines,
But vast brotherhood with true humanity.

The maid who left feeling sorry,
Crying because she misses
The house where they didn't treat her so well...

In my heart, it's all death and the sadness of the world.
All of it lives—because it dies—in my heart.

My heart's a little bigger than the whole universe.

(4/vii/1934)

§

My heart, flag hoisted
At festivals when no one's around…
My heart, boat moored on the bank
Waits for its owner, a yellowing corpse in the rushes…
My heart, galley slave's wife,
Innkeeper in the dead of night,
Guards at the gate, with a malignant smile,
The whole system of the universe,
Sentenced to rot, completed in sphinxes…
My heart, broken manacle…

* * *

§

Music, yes music…
Banal piano from the other floor…
Music, in any case, music…
It comes looking for the weeping immanent
In every human creature,
It comes to torture calm
With desire for a greater calm…
Music… A piano up there,
Someone who plays badly…
But it's music…

Ah, how many childhoods I had!
How many good heartbreaks!
Music…
How many more good heartbreaks!
Always music…
Poor piano played by someone who doesn't know how to play.
But it's music, despite, despite…

Ah, here comes a little more music—
A rational melody—
Rational, my God!
As if something could be rational!
What new landscapes from a piano badly played!?
Music!… Music!…

(19/vii/1934)

§

Midnight gets going, and quiet, too,
Over every part of superimposed houses,
The various floors of the accumulation of life...

They shut the piano on the third floor...
I no longer hear the steps on the second floor...
On the ground floor, the radio's gone quiet...

Everything's going to sleep...

I stay alone with the whole universe.
I don't even want to go to the window:
If I looked out, oh man, what about those stars!?
What great and greater silences there are on high!
What an anti-urban sky!...

Rather, I recluse
In my desire to be no recluse,
I listen anxiously to noises from the street...
An automobile—too fast!—
Doubled steps in conversation quicken me...
The sound of a gate slammed shut hurts me...

Everything's going to sleep...

Only I stay awake, sleepily listening,...
Waiting
For anything but sleep...
Anything...

(9/viii/1934)

§

Sunday I'll go to the park in the person of others,
Content in my anonymity.
Sunday I'll be happy—them, them…
Sunday…
Today it's Friday in the week without a Sunday…
No Sunday at all…
Never Sunday…
But there'll always be someone in the park next Sunday.
So life goes,
Especially for someone who feels,
More or less for someone who thinks:
There'll always be someone in the park on Sunday…
Not on our Sunday,
Not on my Sunday,
Not on Sunday…
But there'll always be someone else in the park on Sunday…

(9/viii/1934)

§

It's been a long time since I've been able
To write a long poem!…
It's been years…

I lost the power of rhythmic development
In which idea and form
Move unanimously together
As body with soul…

I lost everything that made me conscious
Of a certain something in my being…
What's left for me today?
The sun's without my calling it…
The day costs me no effort…
Breeze, a real festival of breeze,
To give me consciousness of air…
And the domestic egotism of not wanting anything else.

But, ah!, my *Triumphal Ode*,
Your rectilinear movement!
Ah, my *Maritime Ode*,
Your general structure in strophe, antistrophe and epode!
And my plans—the plans I planned—
That's what my big odes were!
And that one, the last, the supreme, the impossible one!

(9/viii/1934)

§

Without impatience,
Without curiosity,
Without attention,
I watch you crochet with your two combined
Hands.

I watch it from high on a nonexistent mountain,
Row after row forming a piece of fabric...

What's the reason for the amusement you give
Your hands and soul with this crappy thing
I'd put a spent match on?
And what right do I have
To criticize you, anyway?

None at all.
I have my crochet, too.
It dates from when I began to think...
Row after row forming an all without all...
Fabric, I don't know if it's for clothing or what—
A soul, I don't know if it's for feeling or hearing...
I look at you with so much attention,
I'm not even paying attention anymore...

Crochet, souls, philosophy...
All the religions of the world...
Whatever keeps us going in the night work of our being...
Two ivory needles, a loop, some silence...

(9/viii/1934)

§

—Do you know that old cantiga, Mr. Engineer?
—Which cantiga would that be, woman?
—That really old one. Don't you know it?
The one that goes:
        It rained all night...
—Yes, I remember it, now go away!

—Yes, I remember it.
I have no idea what it reminds me of.
I know I'm reminded right now.
Now, I know I'm reminded of all possible life,
The true, the essential...
        It rained all night
        On all the little fountains
        In the plaza...
I have no idea (o my heart!) what the plaza's fountains are!
But what background music for every being
Was this cantiga for me?
And so then
        It rained all night
        On all the little fountains
        In the plaza...

And me here, me here, me here
So definitively here!
So irremediably here!
Where is that plaza?
Where is that night?
Where is that rain?
And you, Senhora D. Maria,
And you, and you, little red carnation mouth?

I've endured so many fatigues
Full of vague hopes for any kind of a future.
I've slept so often

Under the night sky in the dew of every dream…
I've been useless, shopworn, incongruent—
Like all that stuff out there—life.
I've been all those futile nothings.

Senhora D. Maria,
When I meet you someday,
Ah, how I'll love you!
And with as much love as all who ever loved without a future!
But when does it rain all night
On all the little fountains
In the plaza?
When? And where? where?
Little red carnation mouth!
Was it you, was it you I always loved?
But I never knew your name—I know it now…
Senhora D. Maria,
Little red carnation mouth,
I know you better now, but I'm no closer to you.
I lose you all the more because I found you.

* * *

Porto Style Tripe

One day, in a restaurant beyond time and space,
They served me love as cold tripe.
With utmost delicacy, I told the delegate from the kitchen:
I'd rather have it hot.
I told him tripe (and it was Porto style) is never eaten cold.

They got impatient with me.
You're never right, not even in a restaurant.
I didn't eat, I didn't ask for anything else, I paid the bill,
Went outside, and walked up and down the street.

Who knows what this means?
I don't know, and it happened to me.

(I know very well there was a garden in everyone's childhood,
Private or public, or the neighbor's,
I know very well our playing was its custodian,
And sadness is today's.)

I know this many times over,
But if I asked for love, why did they bring me
Cold Porto style tripe?
It's not a dish you can eat cold,
But they brought it cold.
I didn't complain, but it was cold.
It should never be eaten cold, but it came cold.

* * *

Holiday in the Country

Calm of night; holiday in the mountains;
Calm enhances
Intermittent barking of good watchdogs in the night,
The silence is more accentuated,
Because a nothing buzzes or murmurs in the dark...
Ah, the oppression of all this!
It oppresses, like being happy!
How idyllic a life, if another person had it
With the buzzing or monotonous murmur of nothing
Under the star-freckled sky,
With the barking of the dogs sprayed all over the calmness of
everything!

I came here to rest,
But I forgot to leave myself at home.
I brought with me the essential thorn of being conscious,
The vague nausea, the uncertain sickness, of my own sense of self.
Always this restlessness bitten off in pieces
Like cheap black bread crumbles as it falls.
Always this ill-being taken in evil draughts
Like drunkard's wine when not even nausea holds you back.
Always, always, always
These clogged arteries in my soul,
This lipothymia of the senses,
This...

(Your slender hands, a little bit pale, a little bit mine,
Were quiet on your seated woman's lap that day,
Like another woman's scissors and thimble.
You were mulling, looking at me as if I were space.
I remembered to have something to think about without thinking.
Suddenly, in a half-sigh, you interrupted what you were being,
Consciously looked at me, and you said:
"I feel sorry about every day not being this way"—
This way, like that day that wasn't anything...

§

Ah, you didn't know,
Luckily, you didn't know how
The pity of it is how every day is this way, this way;
The bad thing is how, happy or unhappy,
The soul enjoys or suffers the inner boredom of everything,
Consciously or unconsciously,
Thinking or about to think—
This is the sorry thing…
I remember photographically your still, softly
Extended hands.
At this point, I remember them more than I remember you.
What became of you?
I know you got married in one of life's
Awe-inspiring somewheres. I believe you're a mother. You must be happy.
Why wouldn't you be?

Only because of unfairness…
Yes, it'd be unfair…
Unfair?

(It was a sunny day in the country and I was asleep, smiling)

. . . .

Life…
White or red don't matter: it's all for puking.

* * *

§

I took off the mask and looked in the mirror…
It was the kid from so many years ago…
He hadn't changed a bit…

That's the advantage to knowing how to take off the mask.
You're always the kid,
The revenant past,
The kid.

I took off the mask, and put it back again.
It's better that way.
That way I'm the mask.

And I get back to normal, like at the end of the line.

(11/viii/1934)

§

...As, on days of great occurrences in the center of the city,
In nearly-outlying neighborhoods, conversations in silence at the doors—
Expectation in groups...
Nobody knows anything.
Light trail of a breeze...
A nothing—it's real—
Touches—caress or breath—
What there is till it is...
Magnificence of naturality...
Heart...
What unheard-of Afriques in each desire!
What things better than everything, out there!

On the trolley, my ankle touches the ankle of the woman sitting next to me
With a shopworn involuntariness,
Proximity's short-circuit...
Ideas as random
As an overturned bucket—

I stare at it: it's an overturned bucket...

Hic jacet: I kicked it...

(16/viii/1934)

§

After not having slept,
After no longer being sleepy,
Interminable small hours when you think unthinking,
I saw the day come
Like the worst of all maledictions—
Condemned to the same.

For all that, what wealth of blue-green and red-gilt yellow
In the eternally far sky
In that east they ruined
By saying civilization comes from there;
In that east they stole from us
With their Solar Myth Swindle,
Marvelous east without civilizations, without myths,
Simply sky and light,
Matter without materiality…
All light, even shadow,
The light of night given to day
Fills, at times, irresistibly natural,
The great silence of wheat in no wind,
The shaded green of distant fields,
Life and a feeling of life.
Morning floods the whole city.
My eyes, heavy with the sleep you never got,
What will flood what's behind you tomorrow,
What are you;
What am I?

(5/ix/1934)

Là-bas, je ne sais où...

Right before a trip, that bell...
Knock off the racket, will you?

I'd rather enjoy the repose of the *gare* of the soul I have,
Than watch the advance, the iron arrival
Of the definitive train,
Than sense true departure in the gorges of my stomach,
Than stirrup this foot—
It never learned not to get all mushy every time it had to leave.

At this moment, smoking at the flagstop of today,
I want to stay a morsel clinging to the old life.
Useless life, which was better to leave, which is a cell?
What difference does it make? The whole universe is a cell, and being
        imprisoned has nothing to do with the size of the cell.
The cigarette tastes like looming nausea. The train already left the other
        station...
Goodbye, goodbye, goodbye, all the people who didn't come to see me off,
My abstract, impossible family...
Goodbye, today's day, goodbye, today's flagstop, goodbye life, goodbye life!
To stay like a forgotten labeled suitcase,
In the corner of the waiting area on the other side of the tracks.
To be accosted by the accidental guard after departure—
"What's this? Did someone leave this here?"—

To stay only to think about departing,
To stay and be right,
To stay and die less...

I'm going to the future like to a tough exam.
What if the train never arrived and God felt sorry for me?

Now I see myself in the station, till now a simple metaphor—
I'm a perfectly presentable person.
It's obvious—so they say—I've lived abroad.

My ways are an educated man's, evidently.
I grab my bag and quit the porter like a dirty habit.
The hand holding the bag shakes it and me.

To depart!
I'll never go back,
I'll never go back because you never do.
The place you go back to is always another,
The *gare* you go back to is other.
It's no longer the same people, the same light, the same philosophy.

To depart! My God, to depart! I'm afraid to depart!...

* * *

§

One the eve of never leaving
At least you don't have to pack your bags
Or make plans on paper
With the involuntary accompaniment of the things you forget,
For the still free part of the following day.

You don't have to do anything
On the eve of never departing.

Great calm of there no longer being anything but
What there is to be calm about!
This great tranquility doesn't even know how to shrug
At all of it, think about all of it,
And all of it deliberately come to nothing.
Great joy of not needing to be happy,
Like an opportunity turned inside out.

For so many months I've lived
The vegetative life of thought!
Every day *sine linea*…

Calm, yes, calm…
Great tranquility…
What a rest, after so many physical and psychic travels!
To be able to look at closed luggage as if at nothing!
Nap, soul, nap!
Carpe diem, take a nap!
Take a nap!

You don't have much time! Take a nap.
You're just about to never leave!…

(27/ix/1934)

§

What there is in me is above all weariness—
Not of this or that,
Not even everything or nothing:
Weariness itself as such, itself,
Weariness.

The subtlety of useless sensations,
Violent passions for nothing at all,
Intense love for the supposéd in someone,
All that stuff—
That and what's eternally missing in it—;
All of it makes for weariness,
This weariness,
Weariness.

No doubt there's someone who loves the infinite,
No doubt there's someone who wants the impossible,
No doubt there's someone who doesn't want anything—
Three kinds of idealists, and I'm not one of them:
For I love the infinite infinitely,
For I want the impossible impossibly,
For I want it all, or even a little more, if that could be,
Or even if it couldn't…

The result?
For them, a life lived or dreamed,
For them, a dream dreamed or lived,
For them, the median between all and nothing, that is, that…
For me, only a grand, a deep,
And, ah, with what sterile felicity, weariness,
A supreme weariness,
A weariness supremissimo,
Issimo, issimo, issimo,
Weariness.

(9/x/1934)

§

So many contemporary poems!
So many poets utterly of today—
Everything's interesting, all of them are interesting...
Ah, but it's all so quasi...
It's all vestibulary,
It's all just to write...
Neither art,
Nor science,
Nor true nostalgia...
This one really looks at the silhouette of that cypress...
That one really saw the sunset behind the cypress...
This one really notates the emotion caused by all that stuff...
But, then what?
Ah, my poet, my poems—what then?
The worst thing is always the what then...
It's just that to say you have to think—
To think with second thought—
And you, my old friends, poets and poems,
Think only with the benighted rapidity of blunder—[...] and the pen's—

The consecrated classic is more worthy,
The singing romantic is more worthy,
Anything is more worthy, even if it's bad,
Than the unconstrued purlieus of some good any old thing...
"I have my soul!"
Oh, you sure don't: you have a feeling of it.
Careful with sensation!
Often it belongs to others,
And often it belongs to us
Only by the bewildered accident of our feeling it...

(1/xi/1934)

§

Glory endures down the stairs.
Paradox? No: reality.
Paradox is words;
Reality's what you are.
You went up because you went down.
OK.
Maybe I'll do the same thing tomorrow.
For now, I envy you, most likely,
I don't know if I envy your victory,
I don't know if I envy your getting there,
But I really do believe I envy you…
It's always victory…
Make a package out of me
And then drop it in the river.
And don't forget "most likely" when you drop me there.
That's really important,
Don't forget "most likely."
That's the most important thing.
Because everything is, most likely…

(30/xi/1934)

§

Symbols? I've had it with symbols...
Some people tell me everything's a symbol.
They're all telling me nothing.

What symbols? Dreams...
OK, so the sun's a symbol...
OK, so the moon's a symbol...
OK, so the earth's a symbol...
But who notices the sun except when the rain stops
And it breaks through clouds and points behind its back
At the blue of the sky?
But who notices the moon except to find
Beauty in the light it spreads, not really in itself?
But who notices the earth, that thing we step on?
As for fields, trees and mountains,
We call them the earth by an instinctive diminution,
Because the sea is earth, too...

Well, go on, then, so all of this is symbols...
But what symbol is, not the sun, not the moon, not the earth,
But this precocious debluing sunset,
The sun between ending shreds of clouds,
And the moon up, mystical, on the other side,
And what's left of the daylight
Gilds the hair of the seamstress who stops vaguely at the corner
Where she used to hang out a little (she lives nearby) with her boyfriend
        who left her?

Symbols?... I don't want symbols...
All I want—poor figure, so scrawny, so distressed—
Is for the seamstress to get her boyfriend back.

(18/xii/1934)

§

In memory of Soame Jenyns,
remembered after the poem was written

Sometimes I have felicitous ideas,
Sudden felicitous ideas, in ideas
And in words in which they naturally detach…

After writing, I read…
Why did I write this?
Where did I find this?

In this world, are we just pen and ink
Someone uses to write for real what we sketch here?…

(18/xii/1934)

§

They didn't have electricity there.
And so by the light of a dimming candle
I read, inserted in the bed,
Whatever there was on hand to read—
The Bible, in Portuguese, because (how curious!) they were Protestants.
And I re-read the First Epistle to the Corinthians.
Around me the excessive quiet of provincial nights
Made an enormous contrary clamor
And gave me a tendency to weep in desolation.
The First Epistle to the Corinthians...
I re-read it by the light of a suddenly ancient candle
And a great sea of emotion murmured in me...

I'm nothing...
I'm a fiction...
What am I doing, wanting anything from myself or from everything in
        this world?
"And have no charity"...
And the sovereign voice from the height of the ages sends
The great, soul-freeing message...
"And have no charity"...
And, my God, I have no charity!

(20/xii/1934)

§

No: slowly.
Slowly, because I don't know
Where I want to go.
Between me and my steps,
An instinctive divergence.

Between what I am and what I'm being,
A verbal difference
Corresponding to reality.

Slowly…
Yes, slowly…
I want to think about what
Slowly means…

Maybe there's too much haste in the world.
Maybe ordinary souls want to get here sooner.
Maybe the impression of the moments is very near…
Maybe all of it…
But what's worrying me is this word: slowly…
What has to go slowly?
The universe, maybe…
Truth sends God down to say himself.
But what did anyone ever tell God about it?

(30/xii/1934)

§

The ancients invoked the Muses.
We invoke ourselves to ourselves.
I don't know if the Muses appeared—
That would have depended on what was invoked, and how—
But I know we don't appear.

So often I've leaned over the well I suppose myself to be,
And bleated "Hey!" to hear an echo,
And haven't heard anything more than I've seen—
The dim whiteness of shining water
Down in the useless depth.
No echo back to me...
Only a vague face, which must be mine because it couldn't be anyone else's,

Almost invisible,
A faintly dirty luminescence
There at the bottom...
In the silence and false light of the bottom...

What a Muse!

(3/i/1935—on ms., in English: "First this year"*)*

§

For more than half an hour
I've been sitting at my desk
With the sole intent
Of looking at it.

(Those verses are outside my rhythm.
I'm outside my rhythm, too.)
Inkwell, large, in front of me.
Pens and nibs a little in front of it.
Closer to me, very clean paper.
To my left, a volume of the Encyclopedia Britannica,
To my right—
Ah, to my right!—
My paperknife—yesterday
I didn't have the patience to use it to finish cutting
An interesting book I'll never read.

If only you could hypnotize all this!

(3/i/1935)

§

After I stopped thinking of after
My life became more calm—
I.e., less a life.
I've become my own muted accompanist.

I look, from the top of a low window,
At the girls dancing and playing in the street.
Their ineluctable destiny
Hurts me.
I see a dress half-unbuttoned at the back, and it hurts me.

Great steam-roller, who tells you to roll
This road paved with souls?

(But your voice interrupts me—
High voice, outside, the garden there, a girl—
And it's like I'd let a book
Fall irresolutely on the floor.)

My love, don't we wear, in this dance of life
Made of our natural playing,
The same unbuttoned neckline,
The same gap showing skin above a dirty hem?

(3/i/1935)

§

I, me myself...
Me, full of weariness,
As much as the world can give...
I...

In the end, everything, because everything is me,
Even the stars, as far as I can tell,
Dropped from my pocket to dazzle children...
Which children, I don't know...
I...

Imperfect? Unknown? Divine?
I don't know.
I...

Did I have a past? No doubt...
Do I have a present? No doubt...
Will I have a future? No doubt,
Even if it ends in a little while...
But me, me...
I'm me,
I stay me,
Me...

(4/i/1935)

§

I don't know if the stars rule the world,
Or if cards—
Playing, Tarot—
Can reveal a thing.

I don't know if throwing dice
Can bring you to any conclusion.
And I don't know
If living like everyone else
Gets you anywhere.

Yes, I don't know
If I have to believe in the daily sun
Whose authenticity no one guarantees,
Or if it wouldn't be better, or more comfortable,
To believe in some other sun—
One that shines at night, too—
Some luminous profundity of things
By which I perceive nothing...

In the meantime...
(Let's slow down)
In the meantime
Here's the banister—it's absolutely safe—
Safe in hand—
The banister doesn't belong to me,
It points to what I'm going upstairs to...
Yes... I'm going upstairs...
I'm going upstairs to
I don't know if the stars rule the world...

(5/i/1935)

§

Ah! To be indifferent!
It's from the height of the power of their indifference
That the bosses' bosses run the world.

To be other, even to one's self!
It's from the height of this estrangement
That the saint's masters run the world.

To be forgotten by whatever exists!
It's from the height of thinking about this forgetting
That the gods' gods run the world.

(I didn't hear what you were saying...
I only heard the music, and I didn't even really hear that...
Were you playing and talking at the same time?
Yes, I think you were playing and talking at the same time...
With whom?
With someone for whom everything was ending in the sleep of the
        world...)

(12/i/1935)

I Come Back Home

It's been quite a while since I've written a sonnet,
But that's OK, I'll just write one now.
Sonnets are childhood, and, for an hour,
My childhood is nothing but a big black spot;

It throws me off a train (well, really me…)
Onto a futile and unmoving track;
And the sonnet is like someone looking back
These last two days over everything I see.

Thank Heaven I still haven't forgotten the art
Of fitting fourteen lines together well
So folks will always know right where they are.

Where folks are, or where I am, I don't know…
I'd rather know no more about anything else
And it'll still be bullshit when I do.

(3/ii/1935)

At the time it was written, apparently intended to be Campos' last poem: note by title: (end of the book). There is a very famous poem of the same title by Guerra Junqueiro, in which the poet asks his old nanny to sing him a lullaby and bring him back to his idyllic Portuguese childhood.

§

Yes, everything's all right.
Everything's perfectly all right. But the problem is,
It's all wrong.
I know very well this house is painted gray,
I know very well what this house's number is—
I don't know, but I could know, how they'd appraise it
In the offices they built so they can do such things—
I know very well, I know very well...
But the sad thing is, there are souls there
And the Finance Office couldn't protect
The next-door neighbor from the death of her son.
The Bureau of Whatever couldn't stop
The upstairs neighbor's husband from running away with his sister-in-
        law...
But everything's all right, of course...
And, except for it being all wrong, that's how it is: all right...

(5/iii/1935)

§

I'm tired, of course,
Because at some point folks just have to be tired.
What I'm tired of, I don't know.
It'd do me no good to know,
Since the tiredness will stay with me all the same—
Wounds hurt because they hurt,
Not as a function of whatever causes them.
Yes, I'm tired,
And smiling a little
Because this is all my tiredness is:
A will to sleep in the body,
A desire for not-thinking in the soul,
And over everything the lucid tranquility
Of my retrospective understanding...

And as for that mute luxury—no longer having hope?

I'm intelligent, that's all there is to it.

I've seen a lot and understood a lot of what I've seen,
And there's a certain pleasure even in the tiredness it's all caused me.
I mean, your head's always good for something, isn't it?

(24/vi/1935)

§

I'm not thinking about anything
And this central thing, which isn't even a thing,
Is as agreeable to me as the night air,
Fresh to me in contrast with the hot summer of day.

I'm not thinking about anything, how fine!

Not thinking about anything
Is having your soul whole and to yourself.
Not thinking about anything
Is living intimately
The flux and reflux of life…

I'm thinking about nothing.
Except, it's like I'm lying down uncomfortably.
A pain in the back, or in the side of the back:
There's a bitter taste in my soul:
When everything's all said and done,
It's just that I'm thinking about nothing,
But really, about nothing,
Nothing…

(6/vii/1935)

§

The sleep falling over me,
The mental sleep falling physically over me,
The universal sleep falling individually over me—
This sleep
Appears to others the sleep of sleeping,
The sleep of the will to sleep,
The sleep of being asleep.

But it's more, more from within, more from above;
It's the sleep of the sum of all disillusion,
It's the sleep of the synthesis of every despair;
It's the sleep of holding the world in me
Without having contributed to it.

This sleep falling over me
Is nevertheless like every sleep.
The languor is soothing, at least,
The dejection is at least calming,
The surrender is at least the end of effort,
The end is at least no longer having to wait.

At the sound of a window opening
I turn my head indifferently to the left
And I look over the shoulder that feels it
Through my half-open window.
A girl from the second floor in front
Leans out, with her blue eyes searching for someone.
For whom?,
Asks my indifference.
All this is weariness.

My God, what weariness!…

(28/viii/1935)

§

I'm dizzy,
Dizzy from too much sleep or too much thought—
Maybe even both.
What I know is I'm dizzy
And I honestly don't know if I should get up out of my chair
Or even how to do it.
Let us stay with this for now: I'm dizzy.

In the end
What life have I made of my life?
None.
All interstices,
All approximations,
All a function of the irregular and the absurd,
All nothing.
That's why I'm dizzy...

These days
Every morning I get up
Dizzy...

Yes, truly dizzy...
Without knowing myself, my name,
Without knowing where I am,
Without knowing what I was,
Without knowing anything.

But if that's how it is, that's how it is...
I let myself stay in my chair.
I'm dizzy.
Fine, I'm dizzy.
So I stay seated
And dizzy,
Yes, dizzy...
Dizzy...

(12/ix/1935)

§

All love-letters are
Ridiculous.
They wouldn't be love-letters if they weren't
Ridiculous.

I've also written love-letters in my time,
Like the others,
Ridiculous.

Love-letters, when love's around,
Have to be
Ridiculous.

But, in the end,
Only those creatures who never
Wrote love-letters—
They're what's
Ridiculous.

Oh, for the time when I wrote—
Without even thinking—
My love-letters—they were so
Ridiculous.

Truth is, today
My memory
Of those love-letters
Is what's really
Ridiculous.

(All extravagant words,
Like all extravagant sentiments,
Are naturally
Ridiculous.)

(21/x/1935)

Campos' last poem, written just over a month before Pessoa died on November 30, 1935. In the last stanza, extravagant *translates* esdrúxulas, *which means: extravagant, eccentric, overblown; and also: proparoxytone, dactylic.*

Some Fragments and Short Poems

At sunset, over Lisbon, in the tedium of passing days,
I stare at the tedium of the permanently passing day,
I dwell in passive vigil
Like a lock locking nothing at all.
My passive heart impulsively
Washes up among destitute sphinxes
In consequences and ends, [waking up?] in the [beyond?]...

(1/v/1928)

*

I have no sincerity at all to give you.
If I speak to you, I instinctively adapt my phrases
To a meaning I forget to have.

(22/i/1929)

*

The cruel light of premature summer
Falls out of the spring sky like a scream...

My eyes are burning like coming out of Night...
My brain's as dizzy as if I wanted justice...
Against cruel light, every shape's a silhouette.

(10/iv/1929)

*

This one's a genius, he's everything new and [...]
This other one's a god and the kids of the world spit in his face.
I'd like to be a stone, not breathe anymore, I want
To be a thing incapable of shame or despair,
I was king in my dreams, but there weren't even any dreams, beyond me,
And the last word you write in a book is End.

(1929?)

*

At the end of everything, to sleep.
At the end of what?
At the end of what everything seems to be...,
This little provincial universe between the stars,
This tiny village in outer space,
Not just visible space—, all space.

(after 1930)

*

Scrap soul sold by body weight,
If some derrick lifts, it's just to clear you...
I look analytically, not meaning to,
At what I romanticize, without meaning to.

*(circa 11/ii/1932, the date on the stamp on an ad—for British mystery fiction—
on which the poem is written)*

*

But I don't have problems; I only have mysteries.

All cry my tears, because my tears are everything.
All suffer in my heart, because my heart is everything.

*

And I drop a half-smoked cigarette outside
With no recourse but to light another cigarette

Impatient unto anguish,
Like someone waiting in a station in the outskirts
For the train that will bring ah so very maybe, someone who's maybe
        coming

*

Ah, if only I were unemployed
And didn't have to do anything worthwhile
Except inside me!
To have [...]

(28/ii/1931)

*

What are we? Ships passing in the night,
Each the life of the lines of lit portholes,
Each knowing of the other only that there's life aboard,
Ships, separating points of light in deep black,
Each indecisive shrinkage on either side of black
Everything else is quiet night and cold rises from the sea.

*

Where do the dead rest? Do some
Sleep in this atomically fake universe?

*

In my veins runs a repugnant lava—
Fury of life's horror!

*

A toast to whoever wants to be happy!
Good health and stupidity!

This whole thing about having nerves,
Having intelligence
Or even believing you have one or the other
Has to end one of these days…
Must certainly end, if authoritarian
Regimes remain in power.

(1935)

Translator's Notes

I dedicate these translations to my friends and to the memory of my family: David, Rita and Sara Ann.

•

It has been said that Álvaro de Campos represents the person Fernando Pessoa would most like to have been. Until all of his diaries and all of his letters are available, I will not speculate on the matter.

Pessoa wrote somewhere that, while Campos wrote well, he committed occasional solecisms. Perhaps to my peril, I have tried to reflect this in the translations.

•

I have adhered to the manuscript record as best I can by referring to more than one edition. The punctuation is (mostly) Pessoa's. I have not edited. Anglophone readers deserve Álvaro de Campos as is.

The order of the poems and fragments follows Teresa Rita Lopes' critical edition published in Brazil in 2002.

For a brief definition of heteronymy, please see the afterword to my translation, *The Collected Poems of Alberto Caeiro* (Shearsman Books, 2007).

•

Keith Bosley, Richard Griffin, Edwin Honig and Richard Zenith have produced excellent translations of the Campos poems. I have made great use of those translations and hope that my work does them proud. A number of people have helped me; to list them all would take a whole page, but I must express my special gratitude to David Abel, Ken Bullock, Adam Cornford, Ben Hollander, Andrew Joron, Rovena Mafouz, Erin Moure, Pat Reed and Dan Strongin.

Cher Douglas typed my scrawl and helped immeasurably to make these volumes possible.

About ten years ago, Dana Stevens produced the following translations: 'At the wheel of a Chevrolet'; 'Poem of the Song About Hope'; 'De la Musique...'; 'I'd love to love to love'; 'Great are the deserts'; 'And the splendor of maps'; 'O night serene!'; 'Lisbon with its houses'; and 'Porto Style Tripe'. I have revised all of them to a greater or lesser extent. Dana also helped me with many of the poems at that time, and I can't thank her enough.

Josely Vianna Baptista, Luis Dolhnikoff and Francisco Faria helped clear up difficulties, but they have done so much more than that. I would not like to live in a world without their extraordinary talents, their friendship and their faith in me.

All power to my friend Kent Johnson, without whom this would not have happened.

•

I am all too well aware that half-measures and hasty solutions exist in my translations. I believe that errors are few, but, wherever they exist, they are due to my own ignorance. On the other hand, for various reasons, including stubbornness, I have had to go it more or less alone.

I hope my work will inspire others to do better.

•

Earlier versions of some of these translations have appeared in journals. Many, many thanks to the editors of *Antenym* (Steve Carll), *Five Fingers Review* (John High and Thoreau Lovell), *Prosodia*, *-VeRT* (Andrew Felsinger), *Fascicle* (Tony Tost), *1913: A journal of forms* (Sandra Doller) and especially Roberto Harrison and Andrew Levy of *Crayon* for their support and friendship over the years.

Editions consulted

Fernando Pessoa — *Obra Poética*, ed. Maria Alhete Galhoz, Nova Aguilar, Rio de Janeiro, 1960

Poemas de Álvaro de Campos, ed. Cleonice Berardinelli, Imprensa Nacional–Casa de Moeda, Lisbon, 1992 (critical edition)

Álvaro de Campos, *Livro de Versos, Edição Crítica*, ed. Teresa Rita Lopes, Editorial Estampa, Lisbon, 1993 (critical edition)

Álvaro de Campos, *Poesia*, ed. Teresa Rita Lopes, Companhia das Letras, São Paulo, 2002 (critical edition)

Printed in October 2022
by Rotomail Italia S.p.A., Vignate (MI) - Italy